"A chilling insight into what it is like to survive under surveillance. Lalonde masterfully weaves her experience of intimate partner violence with her years of expertise as an anti-violence educator. Stalking has been a neglected topic in the #MeToo movement. This book is guaranteed to change that."

MANDI GRAY, activist and subject of the documentary
Slut or Nut: Diary of a Rape Trial

"Lalonde shines an unflinching and much-needed spotlight on what happens when women leave bad relationships, but the abuse continues. Both fierce and vulnerable, Lalonde reminds us that healing is rarely linear and almost never final—but something always worth fighting for."

LAUREN MCKEON, author of *F-Bomb:*
Dispatches from the War on Feminism

"Lalonde's breathtaking memoir reignites the necessity of voice. She challenges the conversation around the way we hold and discuss trauma and pens the words with incredible clarity. Silent, she is not, and we are all better for it."

CHELENE KNIGHT, author of
Dear Current Occupant AND *Braided Skin*

Resilience Is Futile

The Life and Death and Life of Julie S. Lalonde

Between the Lines   TORONTO

Resilience is Futile

First published in 2020 by
Between the Lines
401 Richmond Street West
Studio 281
Toronto, Ontario M5V 3A8
Canada
1-800-718-7201
www.btlbooks.com

Every reasonable effort has been made to identify copyright holders.
Between the Lines would be pleased to have any errors or omissions
brought to its attention.

Cataloguing in Publication information available
from Library and Archives Canada
ISBN 9781771134699

Cover and text design by Ingrid Paulson
Author photo by Brendan Brown
Printed in Canada

We acknowledge for their financial support of our publishing
activities: the Government of Canada; the Canada Council
for the Arts; and the Government of Ontario through the
Ontario Arts Council, the Ontario Book Publishers Tax Credit
program, and Ontario Creates.

Canada Council   Conseil des Arts
for the Arts   du Canada

Canadä

ONTARIO ARTS COUNCIL
CONSEIL DES ARTS DE L'ONTARIO
an Ontario government agency
un organisme du gouvernement de l'Ontario

ONTARIO | ONTARIO
CREATES | CRÉATIF

*Dedicated to my twenty-year-old self.
We did it, baby.
We're still here.*

Contents

Note

This book is a memoir based on journals, notes, love letters, death threats, police records, social media posts, articles, and that fickle little thing called memory.

Trauma has a bad habit of messing with one's recollection, so I have relied on the above texts whenever necessary to help me establish timelines and flesh out specific details.

Names have been changed to protect the innocent and the family of the guilty.

Prologue

I HATE THE SUMMER.

While my friends were out drinking on patios and lying on the beach, living their twenties as they should, I found myself hiding in my bathtub. He was always the cruellest version of himself when the temperature rose.

When I was twenty-one, I lived in a small, quaint one-bedroom apartment in a super-sketchy neighbourhood. I worked a crappy retail job for $6.75 an hour while I studied at Carleton University. My landlord was a grumpy old man who wouldn't let me have an air conditioner. It was the summer of 2006, and my apartment was so sweltering that I tossed and turned every night in bed, unable to cool down, wishing for a cool breeze or the hand of God to put me out of my misery. On more than one occasion, I shook my cat awake because she was lying around so much, I feared she'd died.

The only semblance of relief came from leaving my windows open with a dozen fans circulating the dense air. That's how I spotted Xavier.

I had just finished a twelve-hour shift at the mall and dragged myself home, only to see Xavier's car parked outside my window. He was sitting in the driver's seat, looking up at my apartment window.

I instinctively dropped to my knees, hoping he hadn't spotted me yet. I kicked off my shoes and started to crawl across the floor, aiming for the bathroom. There was a window in there too, so I awkwardly crawled into the bathtub and laid my head against the tile. I remember trying to slow my breathing. I hadn't taken a full breath since I got home. From too many moments like this, I had learned the skill of taking several deep breaths to try to slow my beating heart.

I remember lying in the tub, confident that it was the one place in my apartment where he couldn't see me. I closed my eyes and tried to reassure myself: *He didn't see you. Don't worry. He didn't see you.*

Hours went by. I lay there so long, I lost track of time. I'm too tall for any tub, let alone this tiny one. I was so cramped and the air was so fucking hot. I was drenched in sweat but too scared to get out. I was a woman in my twenties too scared to get out of the bathtub.

After convincing myself that he hadn't seen me this time, I abandoned panic for despair. *What had I done to deserve this? Why was this happening? Why wouldn't he stop?*

It's been over a decade since that bathtub. It's been five years since he died. But I still ask myself those questions.

1
Good Girl

I WAS SMART AND EAGER AND WAS RAISED TO ALWAYS BE kind. That's why he noticed me. Years later, when I'd become an established advocate and public speaker, a gruff AM talk radio host asked me what "deficiency" I had that made Xavier target me, and I came up empty. But the truth is, I was keen and kind and that's why he noticed me.

I met Xavier my first few weeks at a new school in a new city. Moving from a town of nine hundred to a school of nine hundred is one hell of an adjustment. It's even more complicated when you transition from a remote Northern Ontario public school to an urban Catholic high school in a convent.

It was the kind of high school people don't believe even exists anymore. The principal and several of the faculty were actual nuns. The dress code was a strict uniform of a polyester navy blue pencil skirt (below the knee), a crisp white blouse buttoned to the neck, and a matching blue vest with unflattering beige nylons and black Mary Janes. In the winter, the nuns were generous and let us wear a hideous blue cardigan.

You couldn't dye your hair an "unnatural" colour or have piercings beyond a simple earring, and men weren't allowed facial hair or hair below their ears. We weren't allowed a spare period and couldn't leave the premises on our lunch break. There were few openly queer students, and our religion class had explicitly homophobic messaging. Every year, the nuns would invite an anti-choice group to picket outside the school with graphic anti-abortion signs. My feminist heart died a little every day for three years.

It was made worse by the fact that my classmates had survived the dreaded grade nine together. Not me. I was plopped into the school in grade ten and didn't know a soul. I was fifteen and all limbs, desperately hoping that I would disappear into the sea of starched blue uniforms.

It was English class and the teacher outlined the books we were to read that year. As the teacher listed the texts we would cover, I realized I had read every one of them the year before. *Phew*. I had an advantage.

When I look back on it now, I can't for the life of me remember the question she asked, but I do remember it was about *The Chrysalids*, a book I adored. This was my shot. I could confidently answer a question. I did and I was right. But I soon felt my cheeks brighten as Xavier muttered under his breath "Nerrrd" like an eighties high school movie cliché. People laughed and he looked at me with the smirk that we teach young women to recognize as flirting; he teases you because he likes you.

I hated him. All I wanted was to blend in, but I took a chance and raised my hand and then this asshole made a scene of it.

It only got worse from there. This new high school had a policy of having people share lockers. They were larger than average-sized lockers, but it's still asking a lot for teenagers to happily share the one space at school that they can call their own. And when you're the new girl in school with no friends, it means having to pick at least one *very* intimate friend on your first day. I looked around and panicked as everyone else paired up and I was left alone. *Fuck.*

I tried to hide my panic but it was obvious, and two girls confidently approached me. I could tell right away that they weren't "cool" girls. They were the type that have long embraced being outsiders and really leaned into it. They were weirdos with weird hobbies and weird names and they didn't give a fuck if you liked it. I liked them immediately. We decided to share one locker among the three of us.

Suddenly, a group of cool girls swarmed me. "You can't share a locker with them. Do you want friends at this school or not?" They proceeded to inform me that it would be social suicide to be seen with the weirdos, and though they hadn't seemed to care about my social status moments earlier, they suddenly took an interest in protecting me. I accepted the new offer.

Having dodged Xavier's mocking and a mean girls' minefield, I thought I was now in the clear. But a week or so later, I heard that I was a slut. I had been trying to keep my head down and focus on learning the school's unspoken customs and social hierarchy. But I'd been five foot ten since junior high and had waist-length blonde hair. I was the new girl in a crowd of nine hundred uniforms and I stuck out in a big, bad way. And because I only spoke when spoken to, people decided to draw their own conclusions as to how I'd landed at their school in the tenth grade.

Never mind that I was a painfully shy virgin. To the group of mean girls, I was a rabid whore who had been forced to move because I'd slept with my best friend's boyfriend and was chased out of town. I was a slut who was keeping to herself because she didn't want people to find out.

The truth was far less scandalous. My dad worked in IT long before it was trendy, and my family up and moved whenever he got a better job offer. But the slut story is what was told and the slut story stuck. I was equal parts mortified and confused.

How do you kill a rumour that is so blatantly untrue? By outing yourself as a loser virgin? I was doomed.

I endured a steady week of side-eyes, whispers, and glares from just about every girl in school. My only constant friends were the two weirdos from day one, who clearly didn't care if I was a slut or not. They'd already learned to be impenetrable. But not me. My skin is porous.

When my dad asked me how things were going at school, I spilled the beans. Ever the practical one, he warned me that someone was going to fight me. They were going to fight me and they were going to aim for my hair, because it was an easy target. "Make sure you don't go into bathrooms by yourself, and if they corner you, throw yourself against the wall so they can't pull your hair from behind."

A violent childhood, a martial arts background, and a career in the infantry gave him some pretty intense knowledge on survival. *Thanks for the hot tip, dad.*

My face, my hair, and my pride were saved not from my years of martial arts training nor from my dad's pep talk on schoolyard bullies. Nope. I was saved by the only woman in school who was taller than me and who showed up to school one day with a cast on her arm. Her boyfriend had broken up with her and she got so angry, she punched a vending machine and shattered her wrist. Andrea was big, bold, and badass and she took me under her wing. When I walked the halls with her, the mean girls got bored and the rumour died as quickly as it was born.

My school might have been on the fence about whether I was a whore, but no one could deny that I held my own on a basketball court. I'd been playing sports for as long as I can remember, and I come by it honestly. My brother could dunk in the eighth grade and my parents coached every sport I played. That first year, basketball was my saviour; I made the team and made friends. For a tournament, we drove six hours away to Ottawa, where I met Jason, a brooding stranger from a neighbouring city. As you do when you're fifteen, I was *smitten*.

It wasn't long before we dated. Long-distance relationships in the early aughts were a serious feat. Bricks for cell phones, no texting. Can you imagine? All we had were embarrassing Hotmail addresses and the "uh-oh" alerts of ICQ and, eventually, MSN Messenger. I once racked up a $120 phone bill yammering away with him for four hours straight. What we could possibly have talked about for that long, I have no idea. But we were in love and stayed that way for the rest of high school.

Jason was taller than me, which is a miracle when you're a tall teenage girl. He was masculine in a way that made my heart swoon, a broad-shouldered rugby player. He wore zip-up hoodies and skater shoes on his size thirteen feet. I loved his shaggy dark hair, his deep, smooth voice, and the way that his bear hugs made me feel small and safe.

A long-distance relationship is expensive and hard on the heart, but it keeps you out of trouble. I wasn't out chasing boys, and I often ran home to log on and catch up with him. It also helped me dissociate from all the drama at school. Shy, introverted, and ever the people pleaser, I was conflict avoidant and did whatever I could do to skirt drama or quell it.

It took me a long time to settle into a squad of high school girlfriends. But being labelled the school's newest whore is always a great way of getting guys to pay attention to you.

Enter Xavier.

Not happy with simply embarrassing me in English class, he took to loudly announcing my name in the hallway when he saw me coming. For a little dude, he talked a big game. Beyond his hallway humiliations, he also insisted on sticking out in every class. He sighed loudly when homework was assigned, talked back to teachers, and muttered his disapproval under his breath at a volume that everyone could hear. He teased everyone and would do absolutely anything for a laugh.

Xavier was a troll before we knew the right term for boys like him. He would goad people for a reaction. At the time, he was simply seen as a textbook class clown who was happiest when all eyes were on him.

Short and wiry, but fit from years of competitive hockey, Xavier was good looking—and not just because the school uniform put otherwise drab young men in well-tailored suits. Xavier had dark hair and strong, broad hands. He had a Clark Kent square jawline and perfectly straight, bright white Chiclet teeth. I've yet to meet anyone with a more infectious laugh. He laughed with his whole self and it enabled his antics. You couldn't help but smile at the stupid shit he did.

I don't remember when we transitioned to being friends. I'm sure it started with me enabling his stupidity with a stifled laugh.

We teach girls from a young age to take cruelty from boys as a compliment. We teach boys from a young age to shroud their affection in brutality. I was not immune. But unfortunately for Xavier, his flirting was not returned. Not for another three years at least. I was very much in love with Jason and happy to have Xavier as my BFF.

Xavier settled himself into the role of friend and confidant. In my view, anyway. Unbeknownst to me, Xavier spent those three years feeling like he had been put in the "friend zone," a purgatory for self-described nice guys who are kind to women but get no sex in return. We were good friends, though. And his character rubbed off on me.

I'd always been a teacher's pet, a keener who took pride in following the rules and getting praise from adults for it. I was organized and painfully neat, and I envied girls who weren't bothered by chipped nail polish and smeared eyeliner. I liked structure, routine, and the safety of predictability.

But my high school was run out of a convent, and the strictness was suffocating. I started questioning the rules and found myself out of my shell and embracing a bit of Xavier rebellion. One day, he somehow managed to rip his tie. The circumstances elude me, and it's pretty telling that I have no idea how a man shredded his thick tie in the middle of the school day—but that was Xavier for you. I took the end piece and wore it as an ascot. The teensy bit of gender bending excited me, and when the civics teacher gave me a lecture about how it wasn't part of the designated uniform and I was to remove it or head to the principal's office, I accused him of sexism. I wasn't actually indignant at the bigotry, but I wanted a taste of the power that comes from talking back to authority.

Xavier taught me the thrill of dissent and we both encouraged each other's eccentricity. He was always down for whatever weird idea I concocted.

I had very chill and progressive parents who subscribed to the rule "If you're going to do it, do it at home while we supervise." I never drank or did drugs, but I wasn't about to waste my parents' hospitality, so I hosted a *lot* of parties. And not content to simply host underage drinking parties, I wanted them to be theme parties. At Easter, I had a Playboy bunny party. When George W. Bush declared war on Iraq, I hosted a "Make love, not war" bash, complete with hippie clothes and psychedelic music. My boyfriend Jason went along with my ideas, and Xavier was always game too. My high school photo albums are peppered with pictures of Xavier and me wearing ridiculous outfits and hamming it up for the camera. We were the best of buds.

Xavier and I once found ourselves standing in front of the school dressed as James Bond and a Bond babe. It was a school event with a James Bond theme, but no one else thought to get a Bond babe sidekick (or to use an old-school "Duck Hunt" Nintendo gun as the weapon).

I had a great boyfriend, a gang of girlfriends, and my bestie Xavier, but I still hated high school. And my home life was no better. My grandmother, at age fifty-nine, collapsed one day at work and was rushed to hospital. It was at first thought to be a stroke, but then she was diagnosed with a hemangioblastoma, a tumour on her brain stem. The surgery to remove the tumour put her in a vegetative state for months. She eventually started recovering but was permanently disabled on the left side, leaving her in a wheelchair.

My family is working class at best, so my grandmother and her dad were living together in a trailer park outside of town to save money. But it quickly became obvious that they could no longer afford her new reality as a disabled woman, and they both moved in with us.

That many bodies under one roof took some serious adjusting to, and there were many months of walking on eggshells. The house was in disarray, we were constantly bumping into each other, and the financial reality of building an accessible addition on our home, feeding two extra people, and preparing for two teenagers in university took its toll. It was a home filled equally with love and chaos.

I wasn't exactly embarrassed, but it did require a lot of explaining when I invited people over: "Yes, this is my brother and my parents. This disabled woman is my maternal grandmother we call Oma, and this spry, able-bodied man is my maternal *great*-grandfather. We all call him Papère. They kinda have their own apartment but we share a kitchen, and that van in the driveway is my great-grandfather's because he drives to the mall every day to hang out with his friends. There's a lot of old people in my house, but they're all very chill and it's okay if you swear or tell dirty jokes. Oh, and Oma sleeps really soundly and my Papère doesn't wear his hearing aids to bed, so we can make noise really late without getting into trouble."

We Lalondes had four generations living under one roof. And it was understood that if you partied at Julie's house, her great-grandfather would make you hangover pancakes.

I survived high school by keeping my eye on the prize. Every year put me one step closer to my childhood dream of becoming a journalist. At seventeen, I applied to Carleton University because I loved Ottawa and my uncle who lived there told me it was known for its J-school. I worked my part-time job at the mall selling sneakers and baggy jeans to white suburban kids who worshipped Eminem. I was saving up for my big move to Ottawa and couldn't wait to pick out bright-coloured Ikea fixings for my apartment.

To make my last year of high school bearable, I committed to joining as many clubs and groups as I could. I won an award for a theatre performance and became MVP of my improv team. I went on a school trip to a ski hill and became a legend—and not because I had any skills on the hill.

I was a very weak skier, but I talked a big game and convinced the attendants to let me ride up a double black diamond hill, mistakenly believing that the more black diamonds, the easier the run. In trying to dismount from the four-person chairlift, I got the binding of my ski tangled. Instead of getting off and taking a sharp left, as instructed, I skied straight ahead, with my head down, trying to untangle my binding. I could hear the Québécois attendant yelling "Madame! Madame!"

Look, I knew I'd fucked up. I knew I had gone straight when I was to go left, but I was trying to fix it. *Gimme a minute, dude.* But he wouldn't lay off. Finally, I lifted my head to tell him off— and flip him off—and as I did so, I felt as though I'd been run over. I immediately collapsed, with no idea of what had just happened. Anyone who skis will know immediately: the oncoming chair lift had smacked me in the face. *That's* why you have to turn left. You dismount. You turn left. The chair lift keeps going, makes a sharp right turn, and heads back down the hill.

The seemingly impatient attendant was simply trying to warn me that I was about to get headbutted by a four-person chairlift. I lay in the snow, with the wind knocked out of me and surrounded by the sounds of "OMG, is she dead? Is she breathing?" I escaped with a massive bruise across the side of my face and the most incredible reason for never joining anyone on a ski trip ever again.

On that same ski trip, a friend confided in me that Xavier had been creeping her out. Since we teach young men that annoying women is the best way to bed them, some men take it a step further and do things like pull up young women's skirts while they're going up the stairs. It was a game that guys at my school took up with gusto, and Xavier was the worst culprit. I always wore shorts under my uniform pencil skirt, so the guys quickly gave up on me. Yanking on my skirt never accomplished the desired humiliation. But my friend did not escape this fate. Worse, it seemed the more she protested, the more Xavier laughed and the more he targeted her.

I didn't identify as a feminist until much later in life, but my politics were already there. I cared about women's rights and routinely called out double standards. I considered myself an ally to women, a real believer in sisterhood. So I wish I could tell you that I came back from that trip and marched up to Xavier to take a strip out of him. I wish I could tell you that I subjected him to the lengthiest, most aggressive feminist rant.

But I didn't. I believed the line about men being awful to women because it's how they flirt. I prioritized the intent of his actions over the impact of his actions. I wanted to believe he was just joking. So I told her to just avoid him. I never mentioned it to him.

Plus, my mind was filled with my own issues. Crawling toward the freedom of graduation, I had doubts about Jason. I loved him dearly, we had been together the teenage equivalent of a lifetime, and he was so unbelievably good to me. But I didn't know if he was good *for* me. He was comfortable with a simple life, and I was so hungry with ambition. The relationship felt like lead shoes. I tried talking to him about it, but what can you possibly "fix" when you're just not compatible? Xavier, my beloved confidant, listened to me oscillate between breaking up and trying to make it work.

The last day of school, Friday the thirteenth, was my eighteenth birthday. I celebrated by getting my first tattoo. It was the greatest day of my life, and because I couldn't help myself, I hosted an eighties-themed birthday party that had everyone in costume, including Oma and Papère. I wore a deep blue dress with puffed sleeves and a side ponytail held up by a tie-dyed scrunchie. Oma rocked a polyester blouse, and the best we could get Papère to commit to was a Cosby-like sweater. There's a photo of the three of us where I ruined the shot with a blink, while Oma and Papère threw their heads back in laughter. Xavier had to work so he missed most of the party, but he showed up late with a case of Dr Pepper (my favourite) that he had jacked from his job at the grocery store and a birthday card he likely also stole.

I felt on top of the world. All I wanted was to leave this shitty town behind and start a new life in Ottawa.

But first, I had to dump Jason. Our breakup was hard and my heart was broken, but I mostly felt sick knowing I had hurt him. Now, I set my sights on living large all summer before I made the big move to Ottawa for university.

Turns out, Xavier had plans of his own. He saw my newfound single status as his time to shine. He had not only loved me for three solid years, with no romantic feelings in return, but he had waited (im)patiently for me to see that *he* was my true love all along. And that's how it started.

It was summer. School was out. All I had was a part-time job and eight weeks or so left before I moved. I was determined to make it the Summer of Julie. It helped that I had all the markers of a good friend. My parents had bought me a 1974 Super Beetle (named June) for Christmas, and I didn't drink. When you're eighteen and you've got access to your own car *and* you're always sober? You're guaranteed to be on everyone's guest list.

Xavier and I started hanging out a lot. On Canada Day, my parents shot off some fireworks in the backyard, and when I went upstairs to get a sweater to break the nighttime chill, Xavier followed me. As I riffled through drawers to find the hoodie I was looking for, he came up behind me, spun me around, and kissed me. It marked the official start of a delightful summer fling that had us hanging out at the beach after dark, driving around in my car, and going to the movies.

I come from a long line of tough Franco-Ontariennes who fought hard for a francophone education. Xavier's French accent and proud francophone family had me over the moon. Jason, bless his heart, had been a true anglophone, or tête carrée as my people say, so having my first, and to date only, French-speaking partner was lovely. I cherished every one of his love letters, written in a mixture of English and French. Whenever we wandered away from bilingual spaces, his light accent was my anchor to my people.

That summer, we made a memorable trip to his cottage with my friend Martine. It was a gorgeous, perfect summer day. I drove us there in my car, and we listened to early-nineties dance-mix CDs. Once we got there, Xavier pulled up his family's small boat and promised to take us to a secluded island. We roasted hot dogs and sunbathed. We hit up the diving rocks and Xavier dared Martine and me to jump off the highest peak. I never back down from a fight, and Martine was game for anything. I still have the video footage of Xavier egging us on from the boat as Martine and I plunged off the cliff at a weird angle and smacked the water. My thigh was bruised black for weeks.

As it got dark, we made our way back home. I dropped the two of them off, but Xavier figured out my parents weren't home and asked me to come pick him up at midnight. He snuck out his window with just a toothbrush in hand and ran across his yard to my car, which was waiting around the corner. We laughed all the way to my house with that nervous energy, anticipating the inevitable.

. . .

WHEN YOU TELL PEOPLE THAT YOUR BOYFRIEND WAS abusive, they paint a picture in their head. I know that picture because there was a time when I could draw it too. We think that image keeps us safe. If we can just avoid men like *that*, we'll be okay.

Xavier became abusive. Xavier became a rapist. But he wasn't that summer. The summer that I fell in love with him, he was none of those things.

That summer night, in my quiet house, he kissed me oh-so-sweetly on my bed and we both knew this was our big moment. I was the only virgin in that bed, but Xavier was gentle and kind and kept checking in to make sure I was okay. He held me tightly, mindful to avoid the giant bruise occupying my entire left thigh. We fell asleep for a few hours before the sun rose and I snuck him back home. I loved him deeply.

But I was under no illusion that this was a "forever" thing. I had just broken up with Jason so that I could move away and spread my wings. No part of me wanted to sign up for another long-term, long-distance relationship.

I threw myself a big going-away party at a campground and invited all my friends. Most of my friends were staying behind and going to the local university, so my brother, my future roommate, and I were the only ones getting a true fare-well. At night, after sex, Xavier burst into tears. He pleaded with me not to end things. "We can make it work, Julie. We can make it work."

I had already hurt one man that summer. A man I had loved. I didn't have it in me to break another heart. He wore me down and eventually, I said we could *try*. "Let's see how things go until Thanksgiving." My gut told me it was a terrible idea, but he looked so relieved.

Just a few days later, my brother and I packed up all our belongings, I grabbed my cat, and we hit the road. Moving to Ottawa. Going to university. It was the Summer of Julie after all!

I loved school immediately. I loved the library, the coffee shops, the student lounges. I loved the anonymity of five-hundred-person lecture halls. I loved being a blank face in a crowd of thousands. I came to university to learn and to become the person I had always wanted to be.

But Xavier felt like he had been left behind. I was having fun, meeting people, and becoming my own person, independent of the shadow of my big brother, the superstar athlete, and my chaotic family life of taking care of my grandmother and great-grandfather. I wasn't someone's kid sister. I wasn't everyone's favourite designated driver. I wasn't Xavier's girlfriend. In Ottawa, I was seen as just another first-year student.

My independence is what Xavier resented the most. He went so far as to insist that he must read my diaries because "we shouldn't have secrets from each other." And not content to simply read my diaries, he provided them with running commentary along the margins as well as a solid twenty pages of his own writing. He wrote about me in the third person, as though he was writing an open letter to the world about how he didn't just love me, he was obsessed with me.

Within the first month that I was away, Xavier visited more than once, and his visits cost me my first job in Ottawa. When you work retail, you have to work weekends. Having to cancel shifts at the last minute because my boyfriend unexpectedly dropped into town didn't fly with my manager.

After every visit, Xavier left in tears and insisted he couldn't live without me. We were chatting via webcam one night when he told me he needed to move to Ottawa to be with me. I panicked. I loved him, but I needed my space. I had school! I didn't need the distraction. But Xavier wore me down until I thought of a perfect excuse. "My parents won't let me move in with you. They always said people shouldn't live together unless they're at least engaged. It's a bad omen for relationships."

I felt like I had bought myself some time. Until I came home for Thanksgiving and was presented, quite unceremoniously, with a ring. The story he told is that he was at the mall food court when he found an abandoned credit card. The restaurant had no idea who the card belonged to and on his way to the lost and found, he realized it was a sign—a sign that he needed to buy me a ring and propose. No fancy proposal for me, but just like that, I had a ring on my finger and no more excuses. Xavier soon showed up at my doorstep in Ottawa.

Our new living arrangement took some serious adjustments. My poor brother had to contend with his sister and her boyfriend sleeping next door. My roommate had to contend with suddenly being the outsider. Sure, the rent was cheaper, but it didn't make up for the extra body that seemed to always be in the way. And he was *always* in the way. Xavier was the antithesis of wallpaper. He had to see and be seen at all times. He was fucking exhausting.

My brother, my roommate, and I were all in school and working part-time jobs. We were busy. Xavier had nothing going on but me. Bored and restless with too much time on his hands, he obsessed over me more and more with each passing day. I thought it would help if he got a job, but it didn't. He was hired to fix computers at a small kiosk in the local mall. Although the job got him out of the house on a consistent basis, it didn't earn me any breathing room. He continued to obsess.

My earliest acknowledgement of Xavier's horribleness came in the form of a journal entry dated November 29, 2003—a little over a month after he had moved in and five months after we'd started dating. My journal entries were part confessional and part passive aggression, knowing he would read them.

"How dare you! You call me a pooper and make me feel like the smallest fucking possible creature alive for not wanting to have sex with you," I wrote. "Why must you take my 'no' as an insult? It's not. Do you think you own me? That the ring on my finger (that you stole!) means that I have to put out 24/7? Do you think I owe you something? That, 'Well I put up with your debates on the media all day long, so now it's time to shut up and blow me'?"

My anger and frustration were palatable from the outset, but as I wrote, I moved from frustration to bargaining. "If something's bothering you, *tell me*. Don't take it out by forcing me to do something I don't want to do. You and me are supposed to be a team. We're supposed to be together. I'm not supposed to lay in bed and be terrified that you won't take no for an answer. You're supposed to love me for who I am."

Finally, I lost all my steam and softened. "Xavier," I concluded, "please wake up and tell me things will be better." This cycle went on for months.

Few of my friends made their dislike of Xavier known to me. And even when they did, it was less "Xavier is abusive" and more "He's so obnoxious—what do you see in him?" It wasn't like people were pulling me aside and telling me to leave him. I was incredibly stealthy and determined to keep things as private as possible. A tiny voice inside me knew Xavier wasn't as nice to me as he should be. But I felt stuck.

Xavier spent months chipping away at me. He took any opportunity to criticize me, put me down, or make me question myself. With gusto. At a time when a cell phone call cost a fortune and texting was nonexistent, he needed to know where I was at all times. He found me a job selling shoes for minimum wage at the mall where he was working. It was how I had spent my high school years, so I was grateful for the easy job, but I soon realized it was just another way to monitor me. Working in the same mall made it easy for him to keep tabs on me. He read my emails and all my diaries, and made no secret of any of it.

It's agonizing to live with an abuser. Sometimes, it's death by a thousand cuts. He chips away at you, piece by piece, until you snap and he sits back with feigned shock, barely covering his smug delight at having succeeded in pushing you over the edge. "Calm down. Why are you being so crazy?" Other times, it is pure waterboarding, a sudden stream of attacks that leaves you so bewildered and confused that you stutter through countless apologies, begging him to stop.

Xavier saw that I had more power than he did in many ways. I was getting a degree; I had a job and big dreams. He would always tell me how beautiful I was and how proud he was to have me on his arm. He appreciated my looks but also ensured that they were all for him.

A new friend from work was a part-time photographer who asked me to model for her. This turned into a long-term collaborative relationship where we took thousands of photos. Xavier loved that I modelled with her but insisted that I never take nude or implied nude photos. Anytime he saw anything remotely risqué, by his standards, he'd throw a fit about how I'd be prettier if I just took portraits to show off "that beautiful face." Otherwise, I was degrading myself. "Don't you want to leave something to the imagination?"

I had beautiful, long blonde hair that drew a lot of attention. One hot summer day, we were waiting for the bus when an older man came up to Xavier and informed him that his girlfriend had "the most beautiful hair. What a knockout." Xavier responded with a smile and a nod, "Yes, I know, she's beautiful," and the man walked off.

Xavier resumed our previous conversation as though I hadn't just been objectified by two men who talked about me like I couldn't hear them. I never brought the conversation up or questioned what had just happened. It was only later that night, replaying the event in my head, that I felt anger rising in my throat. I felt constantly reduced to Xavier's arm candy and made to feel like I should be grateful for the attention.

Anger bubbled inside me, but I tried not to let it show, knowing that it would lead to another fight where Xavier would accuse me of being brainwashed by my women's studies classes. I filed away my anger and kept silent. Soon after, I cut my hair into a chin-length bob.

Xavier would take any opportunity to put me in my place and take the upper hand. Since we were living together and working in the same mall, I couldn't escape him unless I was at school. One day I had errands to run at the bank, and Xavier insisted on joining me on his lunch break. He had left before me, so he hadn't seen what I was wearing. As I waited to speak to a teller, I could hear his "Excuse me, excuse me" as he worked his way up the lineup to meet me. He came up beside me, gave me a look up and down and said, loud enough for everyone to hear, "Why are you wearing those shoes with those pants? They don't go together. You look stupid."

There were so many moments of humiliation like that; why I remember that day in line at the bank, I don't know. But I remember my tight black dress pants and my nude Mary Jane wedges that looked like they were worn by a fifties pin-up star. I loved those shoes and had left the house feeling cute as hell. But all my hot-to-trot youthful confidence drained out of my body and onto the green carpet of the bank as my face flashed red. I don't remember if I responded, but I assume I muttered something about keeping his voice down.

When it was my turn, I went up to the teller. I owed Xavier money for some reason, so I deposited my work cheque and requested the amount I owed him in cash. As the teller left to process the cash, Xavier and I chit-chatted. When the teller came back and counted out the money, Xavier said, loudly, "You should have just asked him to transfer it directly into my account." My face flushed and feeling flustered, I stumbled through some excuse about wanting to see it to make sure it was all there. The teller didn't even try to hide his frustration, sighed deeply, and dramatically turned on his heel to put the cash back.

Why did I cover for Xavier? It was his fuckup. He was the one who failed to mention that he didn't need the cash. He had the time in line, the time the teller deposited my cheque, the time the teller asked me what denomination of bills I wanted. So many opportunities to speak up. But he didn't. And when the error was made clear, he stood there with a smarmy look on his face and my knee-jerk reaction was to make excuses for him.

I always made excuses for him. And when those ran out, or didn't work, I checked out instead. I would become robotic, nodding along, appeasing him, barely conscious of the words coming out of my mouth.

As I got out of the shower one night and came to bed in a robe, he took an MSN Messenger conversation with an old crush out of context and lost his mind. He printed the entire conversation, dozens and dozens of pages, and literally threw them in my face, accusing me of cheating on him.

That night would prove to be my first breakdown, as I tried, to no avail, to explain myself. He shouted over me and kept rereading passages as I sobbed. I collapsed on the bed in a heap of tears and he switched from angry, bratty, wild-eyed Xavier to tender, soothing Xavier. His strong hands stopped waving madly and he tilted his head a little as he approached me. He was sorry for accusing me, I was clearly not cheating on him, he was sorry for hurting my feelings.

He never apologized for violating my privacy or keeping copies of my private conversations. That, he would never apologize for. But he was sorry for making me cry and, as he came to lie on top of me to comfort me, I subconsciously started to flail and push him away. I had never done this before. I felt like a wild animal, thrashing at him, pounding on his chest, trying to free myself from under him. I was filled with a panic I had never known before and desperately wanted him out of my face, out of my bed, out of my life. I wanted him gone.

He pinned my arms to my chest and got in my face, and with a low voice kept repeating, "Calm down. Calm the fuck down." I remember his chest, the feeling of being pinned down, and his voice, insisting that I calm down. But I can't remember his face.

I don't remember what he looked like that day. I know now that it was the first time I coped by dissociating. I was in my body but only partially aware of it. I focused on the heaviness on my chest and drifted away. Drifted to some place other than my bed in my cramped room with my boyfriend sitting on my chest.

The next day, things returned to normal. I went to school, I went to work, and I dealt with Xavier. Long gone were the giddy days of summer, making out in my car and skinny-dipping at the beach. I wanted those days back. Every day, I put one foot in front of the other and tried so hard to get us back to that place.

I knew things weren't healthy with Xavier, but I was equal parts embarrassed and stubborn. Embarrassed that someone like me—someone raised in a loving home with parents who fell in love at eighteen and were still together twenty years later, someone who was studying social justice issues, some-one like that—was allowing her boyfriend to treat her that way. But my teenaged stubbornness had me determined to make it work. No one thought we had a chance. Engaged at eighteen? Such a small-town cliché. You'll never make it, they said. I had made my bed and I was determined to lie in it. *I'll prove them wrong*, I thought.

Some days, it was easier to fake. So many of the things that made Xavier abusive were the flip side of the coin that made him so much fun to be around. Xavier craved adventure, which my more controlled personality found both stressful and exhilarating. He was the most impulsive person I've ever met. His spontaneous nature ensured we never had a dull moment.

Our first summer living together, he got it into his mind that we should go dancing in Montreal. This idea popped into his head at 10 p.m. on a Friday and by 11, we had Martine in the car and were taking the two-hour drive to party in Montreal. Turns out, Martine forgot her ID and most bars wouldn't let us in. Last call was around 2 a.m., so we got barely an hour of dancing in before we had to call it quits. I had just chopped off my waist-length hair and was wearing my best club clothes. Xavier and I were dancing and grinding, my hands running through my new hair that made me feel so sexy. We flirted on the dance floor like the horny nineteen-year-olds we were and everything felt good.

Xavier loved driving more than he liked spending money, so he insisted we drive back to Ottawa rather than getting a last-minute hotel. Martine and I quickly fell asleep and woke up an hour or so later to Xavier cursing that he'd taken the wrong turn, which put us in Cornwall, nowhere near Ottawa. We eventually crawled into the city to the most gorgeous sunrise, and I felt Xavier reach out and grab my hand. It was a perfect night.

Xavier loved cars and lived vicariously through mine. June was my dream car, and Xavier had been one of the few people in high school to revel in my ride. It's unbelievable to me now, but so many people teased me for my '74 purple and orange Beetle. Okay, that's a Herbie paintjob, but she was a classic car and I was seventeen when I got her. *How was it not cool?*

Xavier loved June at first sight. The first summer we lived in Ottawa, we spent countless hours tinkering away at her together. He got me a bitchin' sound system and found a way to bypass the car's existing washer fluid system. Old Volkswagens had an ingenious system of powering the windshield washer fluid by drawing air from the spare tire sitting in the trunk. Since the engine was in the back, the front trunk space held the spare, and a simple tube grabbed air from the tire to power the washer fluid. The problem was that Canadian roads are notorious for their potholes, so I routinely blew a tire and got fed up with grabbing my spare tire, only to find it deflated from the washer fluid system. Rather than spending the money on a mechanic, Xavier rolled up his sleeves and rigged up a whole new system. He loved the challenge of taking things apart and putting them back together, and June proved the perfect ongoing project.

Xavier loved June unashamedly, but never tried to claim her as his own. As a young woman driving a classic car, I encountered so much sexist bullshit from random men and mechanics alike. I would pull into a parking lot with Xavier in the passenger's seat, and men would go up to *him* to ask him what year she was. Xavier would point to me and tell them to ask the obvious owner. He supported me as a woman occupying a man's world but never scolded me for knowing less about cars than he did. I don't know why the car world was the one space where I felt equal and respected by him. He showed no feminist tendencies anywhere else. But cars were our equalizers. My fondest memories of us are driving around in my Beetle, windows down, breeze blowing, bass bumping.

But even on the best of days, I felt like Xavier's babysitter. I once ran into a store to grab a few things, leaving Xavier to wait in the car for what I thought would be a few minutes. My errand took longer than expected and I came back to find my dashboard covered in those labels that grocery stores put on your food to prove you didn't steal it. There were so many stickers, you couldn't see the leather through them. There must have been close to a hundred. When I asked Xavier why the hell he had done that, he just shrugged and said that I took too long and he got bored. My attempts to admonish him would always end with him telling me I needed to loosen up.

The tension between us extended to the rest of the apartment. My brother was partying more than studying, my roommate had a fight with my brother and moved out, and my brother invited a friend to live with us. I became the only woman in a three-bedroom apartment with three men in it. All three guys partied hard, and I tried desperately to keep my head together to do well in school. Pulled in a thousand directions, I was even more vulnerable to Xavier's demands. Between school, work, keeping the apartment together, and trying to get homework done in a house of perpetual partying, I had no energy left to fight Xavier. He eroded me. I was so tired.

When the person you love makes every word a battle, you learn to acquiesce to maintain your sanity. Too exhausted to bother fighting back, you resign yourself to the fact that they're going to win anyway. Xavier never needed to use physical force. He had so diligently chipped away at my resolve that he knew he didn't have to. I would always comply eventually.

One night, I really did try to stand up for myself. He had said something mean, I don't remember what. But I remember thinking, *I'm not going to take this one.* We went to bed angry and I assumed we would sleep it off; we did that often. But Xavier started to undress me and I stiffened. I lay there, frozen in place, and felt myself drift away. *Acquiesce and it'll be over sooner.* But despite my best attempts not to, I started crying.

I vividly remember lying there, quietly sobbing, with my hand on the wall, knowing my brother was on the other side of it. In my mind, I was screaming. *If only I wasn't such a pushover, I could scream and he would come and save me. Somebody save me. Somebody see me.* But all I did was lie there and cry. I was motionless with Xavier's weight on my chest, tears streaming quietly down my face.

When he was finished, he said, "I shouldn't have done that." And despite the fact that we slept in the same bed every night, he sent me an email a few days later to apologize. He never called it rape, but he did have the audacity to reference a sexual assault I had experienced as a young girl and how he felt awful for doing the same thing. He would hurt me several more times but never again bother to apologize.

Meanwhile, the chaos of my party apartment made me fear that I would flunk out of school. I couldn't get work done on campus because Xavier insisted I come home as soon as I was out of class. I couldn't get work done at home because there was always a gang of guys partying hard. The only time I had to do schoolwork was during quiet hours at work. I was drowning and I was scared.

I felt like I was always being pulled in too many directions. I knew school was important and gave it my all. But it became increasingly difficult to do so with Xavier pulling at my sleeve, craving me as entertainment and comfort. He, of course, would never have articulated any of those things. Xavier's preferred method of asking was through passive aggression and manipulation. That man put every Catholic grandmother's guilt game to shame. He would act like a brooding, petulant child until I gave in and did what he wanted, and then he would be back to his laughing, teasing self. The eager-to-please part of me would think, *You did good, Julie. You gave your fiancé what he needed to be happy. You're a good partner and you're making this work.*

I decided that I needed to move out, that *we* needed to move out. I would be getting away from the partying in the apartment, and maybe this would be the jump-start our relationship needed. We found a one-bedroom apartment in a high-rise building. It looked like a Cold War era bunker, but it meant I could walk to school and it was across the street from my best friend Taylor's house. For the first time in a long time, I was hopeful.

But things went from bad to worse. Nothing I did was good enough. I changed my major from communications to women's studies and Canadian studies. To Xavier, this was obviously stupid. "What are you going to do with a women's studies degree? You can't get paid to be a ballbuster, you know." He told me to do something worthwhile with my life. Whenever I came home excited about something I'd learned at school that day, he'd remind me that my work was stupid. "If you want to make the world a better place, you should be a nurse or something. Do something useful."

He would peck at me until I snapped and defended myself. He would guilt-trip me for being mean. He would deny ever provoking me. I would apologize. Rinse, repeat. We lived this cycle for two long, exhausting years.

I wore the fatigue, even though I tried so hard to hide it. Taylor was the first person I confided in about Xavier. She listened, validated, and never once made me feel stupid. Driving us home from yoga class in the spring of 2005, I broke down and told her I needed to leave. In that moment, Taylor saved my life. She turned to me and told me she supported me, but that if I went home and lost my courage and didn't do it, that was okay too.

When I got home and tried to break up with Xavier, I went into a full-blown panic attack and started throwing up. As I was hanging over the toilet, Xavier lay on the floor beside me, rubbed my back, and swore he would change. I wanted so badly to believe him.

It was only possible to survive that moment because Taylor had given me the space to stumble. She'd made it known that the door was always open. I am still grateful for that.

People-pleasing Julie kicked into high gear that summer. Xavier was going to be better, and we were going to make our little family work. He made amends by scoring us tickets to see the Live 8 concert in Toronto. The idea of a daylong concert with acts as varied as Mötley Crüe and Great Big Sea sounded like just the fun we needed. We planned a whole weekend of hanging out with my friend in Toronto and spending a day baking in the sun and listening to a dozen bands. I was stoked.

The day of the concert, Xavier refused to listen to my instructions, and we ended up getting lost. When we finally arrived, a massive lineup had formed. We parked and Xavier insisted on cutting in line. I'm a rule follower at heart and I feared people yelling at us. It didn't seem fair that they had been waiting all that time only to be cut off by a group of smarmy twenty-year-olds. But Xavier didn't listen and snuck his way to the front. Stuck behind with my two friends, we camped out on a blanket and waited for the line to die down. It took forever.

Finally, I couldn't take it anymore and called Xavier to tell him to meet us at the entrance so we could walk to the front and meet up with him, claiming he'd been holding our place. He had gone ahead of us and was enjoying the early acts of the concert, and I was upset to be missing out. We'd waited at least an hour cooking in the sun, so I felt like we weren't really cheating the system. We only cut the line when it was dying down.

As we moved through the sweaty crowd, people let us know we were shitty line-cutters. They muttered under their breath as we walked past them, responding with disdain to our "Excuse us. Sorry. Meeting up with a friend." As I talked on the phone with Xavier and pushed my way to the front, a woman loudly proclaimed to her friend that I was a liar who was just making up a story to cut ahead. Her words were a lit match thrown into my fiery belly. I pulled the phone away from my ear and verbally berated her, making her regret ever being born, let alone daring to speak to me like that. My explosion of rage shocked her and the crowd into silence. My friends looked at me stunned, but no one was more surprised than me. I had unleashed a beast I didn't even realize was in me.

When we finally met up with Xavier at the front of the line, he was cranky and whining like a child. I'd spent hours in the sweltering sun, waiting to get into this damn concert, got screwed over by him, had to unload on a complete stranger to get here, and he dared to be grumpy with *me*, in front of my friends? Oh hell, no. I snapped back at him and turned on my heels to find a spot for us to hang out for the day.

Shocked at the rare sight of my backbone, he seethed all day until it was time to leave. Then he took his power back by speeding down the 401, weaving in between cars, at one point doing 180 kilometres an hour. He'd decided that even though it was now early evening, he preferred to drive the four hours home rather than sleep at my friend's place another night.

He sped into the night, and I gripped the dashboard and screamed at him to slow down, as my friends sat frozen in fear in the back seat. He cackled and insisted it was the only way we would ever get out of Toronto in reasonable time. But I knew it had nothing to do with traffic. I knew instinctively that this was his way of tipping the scales in his favour, giving him control of the situation. I might have my moments of power here and there, but they were temporary and only because he allowed them to happen. Xavier was always the one in control.

But the anger I had unleashed at the concert had only retreated slightly. There was no stuffing that genie back in the bottle. My rage bubbled just below the surface, and I found myself snapping at people who bumped into me on the sidewalk. I was impatient with customers at work. No longer able to filter myself, I reverted to my mother tongue and hurled obscenities in joual at drivers who cut me off, buses that flew past my stop, the jammed DVD player. I was all tabarnac, câlisse, and sacrament; the curse words of my people flew freely from my mouth at every turn. I buzzed with electricity and felt like my insides were hot wires, sparking and jumping. I was furious, enraged, wild.

Try as I might, I can't recall what provoked me to throw something at him. I remember the bright-coloured walls of our apartment. I remember the lime-green couch he sat on, while I stood behind him, near my desk. He was picking at me, slowly chipping away at my thinning patience. I wish I could tell you what started it, but it was so ordinary, so common, so predictable, that my mind filed it away with the rest. We had played this game back and forth so many times. Him nagging me, me protesting and then giving in.

But this time, I didn't acquiesce. I didn't walk away or shut down. I crumpled up the essay I had just printed and threw it at him with a loud scream. He was aghast. But only for a second. Once the shock wore off, he slowly grinned and then started laughing. He looked me straight in the eyes and mocked my anger. I felt my face flush and rushed out of the room, taking a shower to calm down. When I emerged, he didn't even look up from playing Xbox.

On a hot July weekend in 2005, Xavier went away for a family reunion. I don't remember why I didn't go with him; looking back on it now, it does seem odd. Things were tense between us and we fought constantly. I rarely had the energy to defend myself. Gone were the days of even trying to fight back and say no. At work. At home. In bed. I complied and lay there, hoping it would be over faster that way. He would nag at me that he deserved more sex from me, but then, if I ever tried to initiate sex, insinuate that I was some sort of fiend. I could never, ever win.

The news that he was going away for a long weekend without me brought me relief. *A few days of peace and quiet will do me some good,* I thought. *Maybe some time apart will do us some good.*

But SpongeBob SquarePants broke me. A fucking DVD of SpongeBob.

When he left, I noticed my "self-care" SpongeBob movies were missing. Long before we had the option to distract ourselves with Netflix, I would throw on a DVD of SpongeBob SquarePants whenever I was stressed or wanted to shut my brain off. But my attempts to zone out that night were squashed when I realized my DVDs weren't in the cabinet. I called Xavier to ask about them, and he told me he'd lent them to Jessica at the mall. That's when I knew that my suspicions were correct and that he had been cheating on me.

He had been spending a lot of time with a pretty brunette who worked at the Dollar Store across from his kiosk. Xavier never let me go anywhere without him, but he was suddenly spending hours chatting with Jessica and making plans to hang out with her after work. He made no secret of his flirtations and would loudly laugh and tease her in the middle of the mall, for everyone to see. When I tried to confront him about it, he chided me and accused me of being paranoid and insecure. But here I was, on the phone with him, listening to him feigning nonchalance about having lent her my DVDs without my permission. I never said it aloud and neither did he, but we both knew he was caught.

After everything I had endured, after all the excuses I'd made for him—after all that, he cheated on me? That was my line in the sand. To make matters worse, Xavier had left on the last weekend of the month and had "forgotten" to give me his half of the rent. In that same moment, I realized he had cheated on me *and* stiffed me on the rent. I called my dad in tears, begging him to lend me money so I could pay the rent. I don't remember if I mentioned the cheating, but I clearly said something that broke him, because he told me that I needed to leave Xavier. "You need to leave while he's gone. It's the only way. We always knew he was awful. You're better than this. Pack up your stuff and go."

It's clear to me now that I was waiting for my parents to give me permission. Here I was, trying so hard to make my parents proud of me. I wanted their approval so badly, and being with Xavier had made that so difficult. I wanted my parents to think I was smart, independent, and making good choices. They didn't think Xavier and I were going to work? *I'll prove them wrong,* I thought. *They'll see that I know what I'm doing.*

But I had no idea what I was doing. I was scared, lonely, and exhausted. My dad naming Xavier as a problem was the validation I needed to trust my gut and leave him.

I had no money. I couldn't even afford all of our rent. It was dinnertime on a Sunday and Xavier was to be back in twenty-four hours. How was I going to pull this off?

I made phone calls. I called every friend I had and pulled together a plan. I worried that I would need to justify leaving Xavier at all, let alone hastily in the middle of the night. But no one questioned it. They just showed up. Within the hour, I had four friends, a pile of boxes, and a truck and a trailer. We worked diligently through the night, packing up all my belongings, treating the obvious and complicated choices about what to pack with the same level of efficiency.

These books are obviously mine, but did he bring these plates or were they mine? Who owns which blankets? Plants are hard to move, but if I leave them here, he'll kill them. Riding a rollercoaster of emotions, I made the decisions, big and small. One moment, I'd find a photo of us and happily tear it up as my friends cheered me on. The next, I'd find a gift he had given me and collapse on the floor, sobbing uncontrollably.

That night was a condensed version of our entire relationship, a microcosm of our extremes. Xavier and I had the highest of highs and the lowest of lows. We loved deeply and wildly, but when it was bad, it was the worst. We never found a sweet spot in the middle. It was all about excess. We would be on top of the world and I would feel a sense of control over my life, and then the winds would change direction and Xavier would make things miserable. He lived to keep me off balance, always unsure of my next move.

But I loved him dearly. Xavier was the best kisser. He had a small frame but gave strong, soothing hugs. He had a deep love for animals and one day came home covered in blood because he had stopped to try and revive a dog that had been hit by a car. He was extremely close with his great-grandmother, and our visits home always involved stopping in to see her. Xavier never judged my love of uncool music or my preference for a quiet, sober boardgame over a raucous night of drinking at the bar. He wasn't afraid to cry, hold my hand in public, or talk about his feelings—which is rare for a young, straight white guy. He spent months patiently trying to teach me to skate. As I watched him skate backwards with ease, he'd hold my hands and sweetly pull me forward, telling me to keep my ankles tight and my eyes up. He told me every day that I was beautiful—and I believed him.

As I packed up my belongings and said goodbye to the space we had created for ourselves, I mourned him. I grieved for him. For me. For us.

When the last box had been packed, I sat on the floor and wrote a note. I explained to Xavier that this was surely a shock to come home to and it was certainly not the ideal circumstance. But it was what I needed to do. I wrote that I was so, so sorry and to please, give me a few days of space and then *I'll* contact *you*.

My friend wanted me to destroy the place as a final fuck you, but I settled for writing "Goodbye" across the bathroom mirror in bright red lipstick. I grabbed my cat, put the last of my belongings in my Beetle, and drove through tears to my friend's bachelor apartment. It was coming on 6 a.m. when I landed on her couch, exhausted and spent.

I did it.

I did it.

I did it.

I love one person and only one. Julie ███ Lalonde is her name. I am surrounded by pictures of her... Look to my left, there she is on my corkboard, look ahead, she's on my laptop, look to my right, my mirror is decorated with ~~beauty~~ beauty. I've got her teddy next to me and I'm wearing her shirt. She's no longer my girlfriend or fiance, she's an obsession. Usually they're bad, & in his case, I love it. I love her! Her smell just drives me up the wall! She is so ~~so~~ irresistabl

[redacted]

Time to stop that... My wrist is starting to hurt and I'm pretty beat. Long, boring shift at work, talked to my baby, wiped a few tears and I hope I can find a ride down to Ottawa this weekend. It's now 1:35 AM, I told Julie I'd be sleeping but I had to blurt all this out. I'm

I just reread this line: No pun intended!

From :

Sent : May 16, 2004 1:22:15 PM

To :

Subject : I wish...

I wish we could be left alone, I wish I could rewind time, I wish I could take back everything and start comple
wish, I wish. Wishing won't get me nothing because none of that will ever happen.

All I want is us to be happy, to become one, to be left alone and to think alike. Sometimes I ask for too much
sometimes isn't enough.

I don't know why sometime I lose my senses of reality and thoughts and go ahead and do something that I n
do.

A couple nights ago, I knew right then I was making a mistake but it was too late. You pretended not to care,
asleep and I cried the night away. I picture myself being the prick when you were younger. I would never do
but as much as it wasn't alike, it was still the same.

I'm sorry, im sorry, im sorry!

I told you I would change and I did but then go pull some other crap that again has to be changed. That isn't
but it's the fact that I did it to need to realize it shouldn't have been done.

I would do anything to make it up to you after that but I know that nothing will ever be good enough to erase
me so much, I'm always thinking about it, hoping one day you will wake up and forget everything from the pa
start over. You've got a good head on your shoulders and sometimes I don't treat you like it.

I've got more on my mind than I can handle. I back to the pukey feeling in my stomach day in day out. I dor
I just watch you sleep, thinking, is this my last night here? then I leave not to wake you up.

Last night, I took a few trips to the bathroom, kneeling down in front of the toilet not knowing what will happe
disgusted by myself, not to mention, feeling disgusting.

Julie, I desperately wanna be put back on track and work things out. You have no idea what you mean to me

I love you with all my heart and I hope to be able to live a happy life with you, and die next to you at a late ag

I'm sorry.

With lots of love,

xxxxx

over, I wish,

too much

Iy wouldn't

then fell
t, I thought,

2 The Beginning

AS A CHILD OF THE EIGHTIES, I WAS RAISED ON A STEADY
diet of Oprah and painfully earnest after-school specials. A man
in a van with candy or puppies is lurking around every corner.
But be warned, children! There is no candy and there are no
puppies. It's a trap.

d to change

It bothers
we could

eep anymore.

xt. I felt

life.

   As the decade turned, things didn't get much better. The
bogeyman in the van was made real by horrific news stories of
beautiful young white girls being kidnapped, raped, and murdered. Stranger danger had faces in the early nineties: those of
Paul Bernardo and Karla Homolka. I was myself a beautiful
young white girl when Kristen French and Leslie Mahaffy were
kidnapped, raped, tortured, and killed. They had been snatched
up by Bernardo and Homolka, two perfect strangers pretending to be kind.

   A whole generation of girls came of age in the shadow of
their horrific crimes. Our bodies were bait for sadistic rapists,
and it was our responsibility to guard our budding sexuality
with all our might.

I took the "Don't get into cars with strangers" advice very literally and on my first day of school I erupted in tears. My older brother had started school the year before me, and I was so jealous. A keener since birth, I was *very* excited to be starting school. With a green corduroy dress, a bowl cut, and my pink raincoat, I was photographed smiling on our front step, excited for my first day as a big girl. But my dreams of taking a yellow school bus to school were dashed by the arrival of a strange older man in a taxi cab.

There had been a mix-up with the bus to my street, so the school sent a taxi to my house to pick me up. Instead of viewing it as a fancy chauffeur, I saw stranger danger and panicked. I absolutely refused to get into the back seat of that man's car, no matter how much my parents tried to assure me that it was safe. I threw my tiny legs against the door frame of the cab and screamed and hollered until my dad had to drive me to school himself. There's another photo of me, with a big smile and tear-stained cheeks, in the back seat of our station wagon, relieved to be going to the school in the safety of my dad's company.

Well-meaning parents taught their daughters not to talk to strangers and gave us crash courses on how to break out of car trunks. I remember lying on my stomach in our living room, watching an episode of Oprah where they showed children locked in a trunk. They were taught to feel in the dark for the back of the tail light. They were told to scratch, pull, and punch at the cover until they were able to pull the wires free, break through the plastic cover, and frantically wave through the hole. "Someone will see your tiny hand and call police," we were assured.

My mom told me to memorize the instructions. My parents meant well. In the nineties, stranger danger was everywhere, so I never thought to mistrust people who loved me.

As I grew into a teenager, messages about domestic violence started to permeate my world. The message shifted from

"Avoid strangers" to "Avoid abusive men," as though they wore bright neon signs around their necks announcing their presence. Society warns women about the dangers of domestic violence, but it's all thinly veiled victim blaming—bad men exist, but only stupid women love them and even dumber women stay.

What happens when we leave? Leaving Xavier felt so final. I had no idea that the days, months, and years after I left would be far worse than any of the darkest times we'd spent together.

· · ·

AFTER TWELVE HOURS OF FRANTIC PACKING, I CHECKED into my friend Sandra's place on August 1, 2005, around 6 a.m. I had a backpack, my cat, and the clothes on my back. It had taken me two years and two tries, but I'd left him. My new roommate, Sandra, was messy and lived in a filthy bachelor apartment with no bed and a cat named Tenacity. As a clean freak obsessed with tidiness and order, nothing about her dishevelled appearance and bizarre living arrangement appealed to me, but beggars can't be choosers. (Seriously, who doesn't own a bed? On purpose?)

Ottawa was in the middle of a heat wave, so Sandra gave me the couch and she slept on a hammock on the balcony. Exhausted in a way I never thought possible, I fell asleep within seconds.

I awoke hours later to Sandra shaking me awake, screaming at me, "He's coming, Julie! Xavier is coming! Grab your stuff! We gotta go!"

Xavier had come home that morning with flowers in hand, ready to make amends. I'd caught him cheating and a few days apart had given him clarity. He was determined to make things right. Instead, he walked into a half-empty apartment, the walls stripped of all my artwork.

Thinking we'd been robbed, he ran through the apartment calling my name. In his panic, he missed the note pinned to the wall. It was the lipstick on the bathroom mirror that tipped him off. When he read my note, he ignored the part where I told him to wait for me to contact him. Instead, he frantically drove around Ottawa, banging on the doors of anyone who knew me and alternating between sobbing pleas and angry demands. He knew I was *somewhere* and he insisted on finding me.

Xavier had called Sandra while I was sleeping. She'd stayed calm and said she knew nothing. Sandra's parents then called her to say that Xavier had just been by. His presence surprised them, but his wild-eyed demeanour scared them. It seemed very likely he would be coming to Sandra's apartment next.

My adrenaline kicked in and I could feel panic coursing through my veins. We ran down the six flights of stairs, too impatient to wait for the elevator. I fumbled with my keys and struggled to get the car started.

Having a car at twenty years old is a major asset when you're fleeing violence, but driving a flashy '74 Beetle isn't exactly stealthy. I sped out of the parking lot, but I had no idea where to go. Our first priority was to get out of the neighbourhood because if he was coming here, he'd spot my car quickly.

We took a hard right at every red light, too scared to idle there waiting. My hands shook violently as I switched gears. Sandra was on the lookout, whipping her head back and forth, trying to spot Xavier's car. Sandra suggested we head to her friend Tony's place. He lived in the suburbs with his partner and, since I had never been there before, neither had Xavier. He'd never think to look for us at Tony's.

We pulled into the driveway and Sandra ran ahead to knock on the door and explain the situation. Once I was safe inside with a cup of tea in my shaking hands, Tony and his partner joked that they had finished having sex moments before Sandra's knock on the door. They didn't ask me many questions and chatted non-stop about a whole lot of nothing.

"Oh my God, I was so hungover yesterday. That Pride party was fucking wild."

"I was just thinking about you actually. How are you managing without a/c? This weather is unreal."

I half paid attention but appreciated the distraction. Eventually, Sandra and I had to make a decision about our next move. She rejected my offer for her to stay at Tony's while I moved on. "I'm not leaving you," she told me. I wanted to object, but secretly, I was grateful. And I was starting to lose my resolve.

It terrified me to imagine Xavier hunting me down, but I also felt sorry for him. It must have been so shocking to come home to my note. Fleeing Sandra's place, I had initially pictured Xavier finding me and physically attacking me. But I started to think that maybe he just needed to see me. Maybe he just needed me to comfort him, to hold him, to remind him that although we were over, I still loved him. He was heartbroken and scared, and it was my fault.

Tony and Sandra were having none of it. Like stern parents, they started to lecture me on how I needed to stay away from him. Xavier's dangerous, they said; no one in their right mind would do what he's doing. You told him to stay away and he didn't listen. He's dangerous. You can't go back.

As we sat on Tony's couch debating what to do, Taylor called. She lived across the parking lot from the old apartment I had with Xavier and could see from her window that Xavier had come back. The lights were on, and he was pacing up and down the room. But he was home, which meant things had calmed down, at least temporarily.

I convinced Sandra to go home and get some sleep, promising I'd head straight to Taylor's place after dropping her off. Taylor's apartment had underground parking and a view into my old apartment, so it felt like a safe place to land.

After I dropped Sandra off at her cramped bachelor apartment with our two fighting cats inside, I drove to Taylor's house and felt myself getting lightheaded. I looked down at my hands on the steering wheel and realized I couldn't feel them. I watched myself change gears but felt no attachment to my arms or legs. The panic poured out of me and I was flooded with a deep calm. Colours drained away like someone was pulling down the blinds on a sunny day. I went numb and felt myself floating way. Muscle memory brought me to Taylor's house, and as I sat in her living room, watching Xavier pacing in our apartment, I felt nothing.

The nothingness gave me an eerie sense of calm, but everyone around me was frantic and concerned. I decided that the best way to quell the situation was to call Xavier. No one was happy with my plan, but I promised to make the call from a pay phone and to keep it brief. Just a few reassuring words to stop him from driving himself, and others, crazy.

I drove back to Sandra's and spotted a row of pay phones outside the 7-Eleven beside her apartment building. I picked up the receiver, dropped in a quarter, and felt my throat tighten. Xavier picked up immediately and the sound of his voice broke me. I begged him to calm down and told him he was scaring me. Xavier was furious. He lectured me on how my "stupid plan" had been a cruel stunt and said that as his fiancée, I had no right to walk out like that.

As I cried, his tone softened and he insisted he was just worried and desperately needed to see me. "Can we meet up? Please," he pleaded. I told him I would meet with him but wouldn't commit to a date, and told him to stop hunting me and to wait for me to call him in a few days. He seemed satisfied with that, and I hung up, shaken but satisfied that he would stop acting crazy and calm down until I could reason with him in person.

The next day, I took my first real shift at the mall post-breakup. In a retail job, if you don't work, you don't get paid.

I was exhausted, broke, and terrified of running into Xavier. But I needed the money and thought of keeping myself busy as the key to maintaining my sanity.

I wasn't there an hour before Xavier started to pace in front of my store. I avoided making eye contact, but I couldn't ignore him. I was panicking but channelled it into small talk with customers. I talked old women into buying expensive shoes; Xavier paced.

At one point, he walked off and I felt myself relax. Moments later, a fellow mall employee walked into my store with a perplexed look on his face, holding a wilted houseplant. "Your boyfriend asked me to deliver this?" he asked, his confusion turning the statement into a question.

I took the plant from him and stammered, "He's not my boyfriend. He's my ex-boyfriend. I told him to leave me alone. I'm sorry he asked you to do this. He's not my boyfriend." The impromptu delivery man seemed annoyed by the drama of it all and walked off, shaking his head.

Walking to the stockroom to steal a moment of privacy, I leaned against the rows of shoes and started to dry-heave. The anxiety that had been quietly bubbling below the surface all day spilled over, and I hyperventilated and gagged looking at the half-dead plant with a romantic note attached. I realized that Xavier had brought the plant home with him from his trip and planned to present it to me as an olive branch when he got home. Instead, he'd neglected to water it in the two days since, and it now sat lifeless on a shelf in the back of the dingy mall.

I worked a half shift the next day. No Xavier. Elated, I strode across the parking lot to my car, taking a moment to enjoy the gorgeous late-summer weather. It was the home stretch before school started up again, and I was desperate to get my life in order before the chaos of classes. I was still crashing on Sandra's couch—two bodies and two feuding cats in a cramped bachelor apartment. It wasn't helping my situation. My belongings were stored in Sandra's parents' garage, and I felt like I was overstaying my welcome. Sandra and I were busy trying to find a last-minute two-bedroom apartment. I was desperately trying to keep it together.

I thought I had managed to avoid Xavier all morning and was merrily counting my blessings when I approached my car and spotted a note on the windshield. As a classic car driver, I was used to notes on my car ranging from "Nice ride! I had one back in the sixties" to "If you're willing to sell, please call this number." But I knew before I opened it that this particular note was Xavier's doing. My hand shook as I read the letter:

Julie,

I haven't been in a mood to do much. I took the day off yesterday and watched it go to waste. I want to get a few things straightened out. I want to start off by saying I'm not going to hurt you, and I won't touch your car. I'm not like that when it comes to people I love.

I'm not sure if you got what I sent you yesterday, but I'm hoping you took it as a token of love. I bought it shortly before anxiously waiting for the elevator to come say HEY BABY!!! and give you a great big kiss. I had sunglasses for you too, but those are a lost cause.

I just want to get together and get a few things straightened out. I'll let you know that I've had a few people say that they saw you in Sandra's building, and Amanda told me she saw your car in the parking lot. I also traced the pay phone's number to the corner store next to Sandra's building. It was the phone farthest from the doors, nearest to the corner of the building.

He had traced the exact pay phone I had called him from.

His letter went on to explain all the people he had called when he got home and how I was a mean, thoughtless person for having left the way I did. But he wanted to assure me that he would not harm me, he just wanted to talk.

> Anyway, I just want to talk to you. I wanted to leave the flowers on your car and slip a note through your window but I couldn't find your car anywhere. You probably got someone to drive you or you took the bus, thinking I will damage your car. You need to understand that I'm not the way you think I am, you should know that. I have a very creative mind, and could do things NOT to damage your car but cause you a huge inconvenience, like removing your tires, putting them underneath your car, lowering the jack and have the tires support the car. As funny as that could be for a practical joke, I would NEVER do it to someone like you. I would pull something like that on a friend or someone for fun, but not to hurt you. I'm blabbing more than I thought I would, and just have so much on my mind (you're the main thing on my mind). I still love you to death, but you probably have opposing feelings for me (I'm assuming).

I don't remember how I moved from panicked in a parking lot to the floor of Sandra's apartment, on the phone with the police. But I distinctly remember sitting cross-legged on the apartment floor in my underwear and a housecoat, the crushing humidity making every breath unbearable. I picked up the receiver and dialled 911. In a shaking voice, I told them my ex-boyfriend was stalking me and had sent me a letter to prove it. I was scared and just wanted him to stop.

The operator asked if I was safe, and when I answered that I wasn't sure, she followed up with a curt, "Well, is he outside your door right now?" Xavier wasn't outside my door at that very moment, which meant my issue was not an emergency, so she transferred me to the general police line.

Holding back tears and shaking violently, I explained my situation to the new operator. "Did you break up with him or did he break up with you?" she asked flatly.

"I broke up with him on the weekend."

I could sense the annoyance in her voice as she explained that Xavier was young and clearly heartbroken over the breakup. She gave me a case number and told me that should he do anything else, I was to call back and give my case number and they would keep adding things to my file. If the police felt it was worthy of investigation, they would call me back.

Thanking her, I hung up the phone, flopped onto my back, and wept.

I went on like this for a few more days. There were more letters. More pacing in front of my workplace. Sleeping on Sandra's couch, I alternated between complete numbness and uncontrollable sobbing.

Sandra and I were desperately trying to find an apartment for us to share, and I felt like a burden on everyone. I knew my friends were worried and no one had any patience for the empathy I showed Xavier. Whenever I tried to rationalize his behaviour or downplay his letters, friends would cut me off and explain that he was acting crazy.

I was grateful to be crashing at Sandra's but felt bad for dragging her into the dramatic saga that was my life. One day, while she was at work, I decided to clean up her apartment as a small thank-you for her hospitality. I had struggled as a clean freak to live at Sandra's filthy place, especially since I was a guest and knew I should just shut up and be grateful for the free place to crash.

Stripped down to my underwear to survive the unbearable heat, I turned on the radio and set to cleaning, excited for the distraction. I tidied up the floor, shocked at the squalor she chose for herself. Staring at her tiny kitchen, I didn't even know where to start. Dishes were piled everywhere. I started by clearing out the obvious garbage. I grabbed an old Chinese takeout container, and as I lifted it off the counter, I felt something move. I cracked the bag open and saw that it was crawling with maggots.

I started screaming and flung the bag in the garbage. Dropping to my knees, I gripped the counter with both hands and wailed like a banshee. I didn't care if the neighbours heard me. I didn't care if someone called security. I screamed until my throat went dry. Everything felt like too much.

A tiny glimmer of hope came that week when Sandra and I scored a cute, affordable two-bedroom apartment in the building we were already living in. I carried what few possessions I had with me up the stairs to our new place and made plans to get my belongings out of Sandra's parents' garage. While trying to help my geriatric cat adjust to another new apartment, I got a call from police. My repeated calls and the additions to my file had crossed some arbitrary threshold, and the police finally felt that my case was deserving of some attention.

An officer called me to run over the details again. He asked for Xavier's number and told me that in his experience, a simple phone call from police is usually enough to scare these people straight. I was told to sit tight and wait to hear from him again. Not ten minutes later, the officer called me back and recounted how Xavier had picked up right away and sobbed into the phone, saying his actions were born from a deep sadness and heartbreak. "He cried, Julie," the officer explained. "He's obviously really upset. So I wouldn't worry about him. He won't be calling you again." The officer was clear that one phone call would do the trick, but if Xavier ever contacted me again, I should notify police right away.

I hung up the phone and, before I had a moment to process, it immediately rang again with Xavier screaming into the receiver that I was ruining his life and getting him in trouble. He had cried to police, heard their demand to leave me alone, and then spent the next five minutes calling my number incessantly until the line freed up. I wish I could tell you that I hung up on his ass and called the police right away. I want so badly to tell you that this violation unleashed a deep rage inside me. But I can't.

Xavier yelled into the phone that I was a dramatic bitch, and I felt myself shut down. My arms went numb, my legs turned to stone. I listened to Xavier drone on and asked him what I should do to make things right. I just wanted everything to stop. And it was clear that the only person with the power to do that was the man yelling at me on the phone.

I hung up.

I didn't notify the police.

I didn't tell anyone what happened.

I got into my car and went to meet Xavier.

Thinking I could strike a balance between staying safe and appeasing him, I told him to meet me at a coffee shop nearby. It felt safest to meet in public. But I didn't make it out of my car before he spotted me, grabbed me by the arm, and dragged me into his car. Between tears, he told me how he was so hurt and wanted me to come back.

I sat frozen in place, staring straight ahead. I was mortified. His pathetic cries were embarrassing to watch. I hated myself for being so weak and unable to extricate myself from him.

I had left my engagement ring behind when I fled, but he reached across the car, grabbed my hand, and slipped the ring back on. Before long, I was back in my car, following him to our old apartment.

What he said to convince me to come back escapes me now. My memories of that night are flashes of colour in a black-and-white movie. Scrubbing the lipstick-stained mirror in the bathroom while he hovered over my shoulder. Petting our two birds that I had left behind.

I hated myself for going into the bedroom. I hated the blackout curtains and the hideous comforter. I hated the stifling air and the mess he had made in a room that I had proudly kept spotless for us.

He asked me if he could fuck me and didn't wait for a response. I balled up the duvet in my fists, buried my face, and cried softly, hating myself. It should have hurt, but I felt nothing but the rough blanket against my cheek as he hammered into me, splitting my life in two.

I did this to myself. I knew he was poison but I drank him anyway.

I went home and told no one.

The next day, Xavier met me at Sandra's parents' place and loaded my belongings into his car. He was going to help me settle into my new apartment and wanted to help me avoid the cost of a U-Haul rental. Sandra's parents shook their heads at me as I quietly packed up my things, avoiding eye contact. I was mortified and knew everyone was drawing conclusions. I had either exaggerated Xavier's awfulness or I was stupid enough to go back for more abuse.

Xavier had decided that we were just on a break. We would continue to live apart, but we would work on our relationship and eventually get back together. I let him believe this because I thought it would keep me safe.

I was wearing on everyone's patience. My friends, my roommate, my colleagues, and my parents did little to hide their disappointment in me. When I was terrified of running into him, they understood. But letting him in baffled them. We had all been raised on the same messages. They could spot the bad man. Why couldn't I?

I slowly became friends with Sandra's brother, Tom. A tall, broad-shouldered gentle giant, he seemed kind and sympathetic. I was completely unable to be alone, and so I invited him out for lunch one day. Munching on chicken salad at the Swiss Chalet beside the mall where I worked, we talked about our favourite movies and stand-up comedians. He seemed genuinely interested in what I was studying and listened as I talked about my upcoming course load. I appreciated having a new friend and revelled in the opportunity to talk about anything other than my imploded love life.

Days later, Tom sent me a flirty message on MSN Messenger. I was taken aback and politely declined his advances, telling him I wasn't interested in dating right now. He was irate and accused me of leading him on by inviting him to lunch. I was stunned. I asked him if he had only helped me get away from Xavier because he wanted to fuck me. "Of course," he replied. "Why else do you think I put up with all that bullshit?" I felt so stupid.

Xavier continued to weasel his way into my life. I tried to hold the line, but he found excuses to be in my orbit and guilt-tripped or manipulated me into letting him in. Ottawa's heat wave raged on, and I had no money for an air conditioner. On one particularly sweltering day, Xavier knocked at my door and convinced me to come by and watch a movie. "C'mon. It's like, two hours. Max. And you can sit right beside the air conditioner and soak it all in," he suggested.

Every time I walked back into that old apartment I had sworn to leave behind just a few weeks before, I hated myself on a level I had never thought possible. Sitting on the old couch, drinking from the old glasses, looking out the old windows, I sank deeper and deeper into self-loathing. My newly developed internal refrain would start up the second I crossed the threshold into that stale apartment. *Why are you doing this? You fucking idiot. Why are you here?*

I don't remember what we watched. But when it was over, I was grateful that I had survived a few hours without being pressured into making out with him. We had sat side by side on the couch like awkward old friends. Him bubbly and chatty, me giving him one-word answers, pretending to be invested in the plot of the movie. As I gathered up my things to make a hasty exit, he came around the corner, pulling the mattress and blankets behind him like a *Peanuts* character.

He looked like a true man-child and I was caught so off guard that I burst out laughing. "Dude, what the fuck are you doing?" I asked between giggles.

"I thought we could lay down for a bit and just talk," he smiled back at me. "It's too hot in the bedroom so I thought we'd set up camp out here. Just for a bit! I swear."

My mind goes blank at how I ended up on the mattress, but we must have talked long enough that the weight of the conversation combined with the oppressive heat put me to sleep. I don't know how long I lay there. I don't know if he even fell asleep at all. My eyes fluttered awake and I became aware that my surroundings had changed. My chest was exposed and my legs were being crushed. I adjusted my eyes and realized that Xavier was staring straight at me with a look I didn't recognize. He looked straight-up crazy. He was wide-eyed and motionless other than his right arm, which appeared to be moving in a motion whose purpose I soon recognized. He was jerking off on me.

Xavier was a rapist. He had sexually assaulted me in various humiliating ways for years. But this was new.

Xavier liked his sex *very* vanilla. Almost always missionary. Always in a bed. He didn't like sex toys or dirty talk. He wasn't into spanking or role play. He was far more sexually experienced than I was, but I realized early into our relationship that our tastes differed. Anytime I had tried to suggest spicing things up, he shot me down.

But here he was. Doing this.

I was bigger than him. My arms weren't pinned. I could have bucked him off me. I could have reached up and punched him out. I knew all this. But instead, I crossed my arms across my eyes and tensed every muscle in my body.

"Happy now, you fucking whore?" he spat at me as he dismounted and pulled up his shorts. His words stung, but I didn't want to give him the satisfaction of seeing me cry. I sat up, buttoned my shirt back up, and left the apartment without saying a word. I caught a glimpse of myself in the elevator's mirror. My matted hair and soaked shirt made me look so trashy, like a clichéd girl on a walk of shame.

We never spoke of what happened. I buried the secret deep with all the other secrets and my hatred of myself.

But he kept contacting me, and although part of me wanted him out of my life completely, I felt so helpless. He had me constantly on my heels and all because I had dared to show him an iota of kindness. My friends were getting exasperated. Xavier was slowly isolating me, and I was completely oblivious. I was alone and exhausted, which made it easier for him to convince me that I needed his help.

School was starting up soon and it was a welcome distraction to prepare for classes. My new apartment with Sandra was sparse. Xavier insisted on helping me get settled, so we drove to Ikea, where we looked like a normal couple shopping for back-to-school specials. I had been sleeping on the couch, so I was excited to finally have a bed of my own. Since Xavier had already figured out where I lived, I thought there was no harm in inviting him into my apartment. The warm weather raged on, and he sat on the floor, Allen key in hand, and diligently assembled my new life.

As we put up shelves and built my new bed, time ran away from me. I realized I was going to be late for work. I tried to shoo Xavier out of my apartment, but he insisted that he was almost done and suggested I go on to work and leave him behind to finish.

He had been so kind to me for the past few days, and although I never fully trusted him, I had let my guard down again. My plan of playing nice and feigning interest in reconciliation seemed to be working. I figured there was no harm in leaving him alone in my apartment as I dashed off to work.

I came home that night to an assembled bed, complete with fresh new sheets, and the realization that he had printed every personal file he could find on my computer. I was a prolific poet. I had churned out hundreds of poems in my short life. I had even won a poetry contest as an angst-ridden teen. I never fancied myself particularly talented, but I loved the act of writing.

While I was at work, trusting that Xavier was simply assembling my furniture, he had instead been printing over a hundred pages of poetry, private writings, and MSN Messenger chat transcripts. He assembled my bed, violated my privacy, took the documents with him, and left my apartment, locking the door behind him. He was technologically savvy and a sneaky bastard, but this time he had been sloppy and had left the printer prompt screen open on my laptop, which is what tipped me off.

The violation felt like a punch in the throat. *How could I have been so stupid?* He had already done so many heinous things and shown himself untrustworthy. I was furious with him but mad at myself for being so naive. And who was I going to tell? I had willingly let Xavier into my apartment when everyone was so quick to remind me that he was bad news. This was my fault. I had trusted him, and in turn, he had betrayed me.

When I confronted him about the poetry, he was nonplussed. "Why should we have secrets from each other?" he insisted. No matter how many different ways I tried to explain it to him, he refused to see it from my perspective.

Perhaps it was because my writing was so intimate. Perhaps I was projecting how disappointed I was in myself. But I decided to cut him off again.

After a brief discussion with my manager, I determined that the next course of action would be an injunction from mall security that would ban him from entering my store. Since Xavier worked at the same mall as me, I couldn't ban him from the whole place. But my employer did have control over our particular location. It wasn't much, but it would guarantee that

I'd be free of him at least thirty-five hours a week.

Because the mall was so small and rundown, everyone who worked there shared in the misery of long days with few customers. It wasn't unusual for a group of us to congregate in the middle of the mall, only half watching our stores as we chatted to pass the time. We created nicknames for regular customers. There was Pirate, the homeless woman with an eye patch who pushed a shopping cart around all day, and T-Rex, a boy who likely had Tourette's syndrome who would yell "Dinosaur!" over and over as his dad shopped the mall. We had the morning mall walkers who showed up before stores even opened, and the group of older Lebanese men who would sit at the coffee shop for hours. We shared inside jokes and stayed busy by keeping up on all the mall drama.

Naturally, the situation between Xavier and me was no secret, and alliances were quickly formed. At the north end of the mall, where I worked, people were on team Julie, horrified by the sight of Xavier pacing in front of my store. The south end is where Xavier worked. He had convinced the women there that I was a crazy, heartless bitch who kept leading him on, just to stomp on his heart again.

When south-end staff got wind that I was trying to ban Xavier from my store, they wasted no time in alerting him. Furious, he marched up to the mall management's office on the second floor and calmly explained that we were just having a bit of a rough patch in our relationship but that we were very much together. My attempts to ban him were a petty power move, not a reflection of any real danger. He informed them that we were still sleeping together, so how could I possibly be afraid of him?

Xavier spun a believable tale, and within an hour, mall management was handing me a formal letter informing me that my request for an injunction had been denied and that they would be contacting the owner of my store to suggest that I be fired for wasting everyone's time. I snapped, which only served to further Xavier's point that he was cool, calm, and collected and I was some unhinged Jerry Springer guest, stirring up drama for fun.

Shaking with anger, it was now my turn to call Xavier and yell at him. In an impressive mixture of English and joual, I told him he was a lying piece of shit and a real asshole for costing me my job. "Tabarnac, c'est quoi ton esti d'problème? You know I need this job and you're gonna fuck me over like this? Va chier, Xavier! Va chier!" He seemed genuinely surprised that mall management would retaliate against me and asked to meet with me so he could apologize. Refusing to fuel the rumour mill at work, I told him to meet me across the street in the Toys "R" Us parking lot at 9 p.m.

I closed up the till, swept the floors, and banged the security doors shut. I drove across the street, filled with irrepressible rage. I pulled my car up beside Xavier's, jumped out, and unleashed on him in a hushed tone. I was pissed, but I was also hyperaware that the parking lot was emptying out, and I didn't want to feed the narrative that I was dramatic white trash. Xavier leaned back against his car, pinned to the door by my stream of expletives. I was angry and it felt *good*. He insisted that he was only trying to defend himself against my attacks.

The parking lot cleared as we exchanged quiet barbs back and forth, until I saw out of the corner of my eye that someone was walking straight toward us. As he got closer, I saw he was wearing a Toys "R" Us smock. I thought, *Oh shit. We're about to be escorted off the premises.*

Tall and skinny with long hair, he looked to be about our age. "Is this a bad time?" he asked me in a surprisingly casual tone. Before I could answer, Xavier piped in. "We're obviously busy, dude. Leave us alone." The Toys "R" Us employee was having none of it. He could tell something was up, so turning to look at me, he said over his shoulder, "I wasn't talking to you, buddy."

It then dawned on me that he wasn't here to kick us out. He was here to help. "Is that your car?" asked my new friend. "I drive an old Beetle, too!"

Relieved for the distraction and pumped to talk with a fellow classic car driver, I excitedly told him that yes, this was my baby, her name was June and she was a '74 Super Beetle. He told me about his '76 Beetle, which was a real beauty but a real pain in the ass. Hence he'd named her Christine, after the Stephen King novel. He extended his hand, all the while ignoring a fuming Xavier. "I'm James. So cool to meet you. What's your name?"

Under his shaggy hair, I could make out green eyes, full lips, and perfect pearly white teeth. (I'm a sucker for good dentistry.) Sensing he was on borrowed time, he started to back away, but not without first asking me if I had a good mechanic. "No!" I replied. "And it's been two years of living here. I'm getting pretty desperate, to be honest."

He asked for my email and said he would put me in touch with his guy, a local legend in the air-cooled world. Grateful for the momentary distraction and the new mechanic contact, I bid adieu to my new friend as he strode off.

Pouting that he had been ignored for a whole five minutes, Xavier quickly picked up where we'd left off and started berating me for reporting him to my manager, choosing to ignore that whole trying-to-get-me-fired thing. We went back and forth for another while, until he agreed to contact mall management the next day to tell them to back off. I said thank you and we went our separate ways.

I kept my job but I also lost any ability to control him at work. He kept pacing in front of my store. The letters continued. He showed up unannounced at my apartment. He followed me around campus. Every day, I added things to my police file.

On an otherwise ordinary day, Xavier was on his worst behaviour. He called non-stop, then came to my apartment with flowers and demanded to be let in. I called the police multiple times that day, stating each time matter-of-factly what had just happened.

"You've called five times today," the operator responded, sounding annoyed.

"Oh, have I? I don't know. I was told to call every time he did something. Should I stop calling?" I stammered, feeling shy and self-conscious.

"No, you're supposed to call. You're doing the right thing. I just can't understand why you've called so many times and the police have never come to take a statement. Do you have a peace bond?"

I was twenty years old. I'd never studied law. I didn't even know a lawyer. I had no clue what a peace bond was. She proceeded to explain to me that a peace bond, commonly referred to as a restraining order, was a "recognizance to keep the peace." It was something I could request on my own, without involving the police. I just needed to present my case to an agent at the courthouse and Xavier would be legally required to stay the hell away from me. I was elated.

Thinking this woman had just given me all the gems she could, I started to wrap up the call and was making mental notes on the logistics of getting a peace bond when she interrupted my polite thank yous with a question. "Do you want the police to take a statement? Do you want them to formally investigate him?"

"Of course," I replied. "But it's been weeks since I called them and I haven't heard anything, so I kinda assumed it wasn't a priority for them."

She then calmly explained to me that I should hang up the phone and call 911, saying that Xavier was on his way to get me. "If you don't make it sound like he's literally outside your door, they won't come. You won't register as a priority unless you make it sound urgent."

I was stunned that an operator with the police was instructing me on how to play the system to get what I needed. Grateful for the hot tip but also shocked at what I needed to do, I hung up the phone and panicked. It was now late in the day and my mind was spinning. She had told me to call right away with a sense of urgency, but the reality of what I had to do scared me. Did I really want to kick things up a notch? The last time the police had gotten involved, Xavier had turned up the volume on his tormenting. Did I want that again?

We had been living this cycle where I ignored him, then was kind to him, then got angry with him, and then cut him off again. I had been ignoring him for a few days and could feel myself softening. *Was he really that bad?* Maybe this was just a really bad day and he was going to calm down again.

I wanted so badly to believe it was all temporary. I just wanted it to be over.

msn Hotmail

From :	
Sent :	August 21, 2005 8:08:39 PM
To :	
Subject :	Julie...

Julie, I don't know why you gotta be this way, but I don't like it. Apparently a friend of m everything you use online, and came across what's below this message. He changed all t you want it, I'll gladly return it, but I still wonder why you're being this way... I've been s return *throws confetti*.

I also told him to leave you this email... Wasn't that nice...

I'm still thinking.... And I realized that I may have scared you with the info that I said in the last letter.

THAT WAS NOT MY INTENTION. I have no one to talk to, I am lonely, and I just want to let you know that I am constantly thinking of you, and how people are telling me where they see you, and since that's all I think of, I am putting everything together.

I don't want you to keep running. I know you told me to leave you alone, and not try to find you... And honestly, I haven't gone out looking for you. I didn't go looking for your car in the parking lot, you need to believe me on this. I am respecting what you asked. My wheels in my head are just spinning in high gear and from everything I hear, I'm just putting it together like a puzzle, without wanting to.

I could have just pretended not to know anything, but I thought I'd share it with you. I am not trying to say "I'll hunt you down wherever you go, cause you'll never be able to hide from me". I am not stalking you. I don't even know if any of my suspicions are true. Someone could tell me that they saw your car in the St-Laurent Mall parking lot at 2am and I would piece that together, and come up with something like you're spending the nights in parking lots, sleeping in your car.

Just wanted to clarify that I AM NOT STALKING YOU, I AM NOT FOLLOWING YOU, I AM RESPECTING WHAT YOU ASKED FOR and that I only said those things because I don't want you to think that I am plotting anything because I am not.

I also want to say again I AM NOT GOING TO HURT YOU OR YOUR CAR.

I love you, and I would still do anything to make sure you are safe, whether it's what you want or not. I want you to be safe. I care for you more than anything or anyone.

I'm really repeating myself, because I'm too brain dead right now to put something together that makes proper sense... Sadly, I don't remember what I was just going to write. So much for this paragraph.

I hope to see you soon, and I hope to one day, straighten things out and sew our teddy bears back together, he's lonely too.

With ALL my love,

with plenty of talent) got a hold of
asswords, and I have the list. If
e to you, and I get shat on in

3
Trauma on Trial

I'm not here "looking" for you... I needed to go to the bank... The car is sold. Please accept these flowers. They are the one I brought home last night.

♡ ▮▮▮▮

I WAS NINE YEARS OLD THE FIRST TIME I SAW A COP IN real life. My friend Mélissa and I had spent all night rewatching the same shitty movies we loved to binge on our sleepovers. *Drop Dead Fred* was a favourite. We'd seen it so many times, we knew it by heart.

Our movie watching at Mélissa's place was often preceded by channel surfing, which I loved because my hippie parents disapproved of cable. If we were lucky, we'd stay up late enough to catch some *Bleu Nuit*, a softcore porn show from Quebec that was the source of many sexual awakenings among Canadian kids in the early nineties. We would lie on our stomachs on the floor of her basement and giggle through the sex scenes, pretending to be horrified but loving every minute.

Mélissa was a school friend who played on my baseball team. Although we lived across town from each other, we had frequent sleepovers. She lived with her mom and baby sister on the end unit of a block of low-income row houses with a creek in her backyard.

I was mesmerized by this house of women. Her mom had that stunning, lithe look that was popular in the grunge era. She was like a small-town, Indigenous version of Winona Ryder. She had a faraway look in her eyes and loved to rock belly tops and short shorts. She had a manic, high-energy vibe about her, and I thought she was so cool.

Mélissa and I would sneak upstairs for snacks during sleepovers and be met with a giant cloud of blue smoke, as her mom and heavily tattooed men chain-smoked and played cards until the wee hours of the morning. I routinely fell asleep in her basement to the sound upstairs of raucous laughter, dirty jokes, and swearing.

Mélissa and I were lazily rising from our slumber in the basement one Sunday when we heard the doorbell ring. We ran upstairs to answer it and were met by her mother blocking the way. Peeking behind her, we could see a uniformed police officer standing in the door. He filled the entire door frame and did not look happy. She shooed us back down the stairs and told us to stay away. As she turned to head back to the door, we crouched around the corner, so we were out of sight but still within earshot.

Mélissa hung her head low with her arms wrapped around her knees, tapping her foot. I sat beside her, terrified. My parents had a lot of cops on their baseball team, but I never saw them in uniform. I just saw them in baseball jerseys, drinking beer on the sidelines, cracking jokes. A real police officer with a gun and a bulletproof vest was something I had only ever seen in movies. My little brain couldn't believe what was happening.

We listened as the officer grilled Mélissa's mom about the whereabouts of her grandmother. It seemed Mélissa's grandmother had pissed off the cops by filing a police report about an abusive boyfriend, later revoking her request and then skipping town. The cop's voice was steady but forceful. He suspected that Mélissa's mom not only knew the grandmother's whereabouts but was actively hiding her. But she was having none of it. She was firing back, loudly and aggressively. She didn't know where her mother was, but even if she did, she wasn't going to tell him. She was spitting fire, telling him to return with a warrant or get the fuck out of her house.

I was stunned. I felt myself flush, realizing for the first time why Mélissa didn't share my excited energy. She had seen this scene before and was humiliated that I was a witness. Eventually, the cop left with a stern promise that he would be back. When we heard her mother slam the door, we scurried down the stairs to the basement, hoping she hadn't noticed our eavesdropping. We were two little girls faced with adult problems, so we processed it the best way we knew how—by ignoring the obvious and playing Barbies while we listened to a Céline Dion tape.

Ten years later, I called the police and told them I was afraid. Sporting a tie-dyed Mickey Mouse T-shirt I'd had since the fifth grade and two pigtails, I hadn't consciously picked out the most juvenile ensemble I owned, but I looked much younger than my twenty years when I answered the door to two uniformed officers. I had taken the operator's advice to work the system by calling 911 and saying I thought Xavier was on his way to hurt me. Shortly after the call, two officers filled my doorway. The female officer asked if she could come in, while the male officer scanned up and down the halls. They were serious but polite and gave no indication of disbelief.

It had been a long time since I had seen police in the flesh, and a lot had changed. I was no longer a wide-eyed, naive little girl crouching in a stairwell. I was a solid two years into a women's studies degree, so I knew enough about systemic responses to violence against women to be cautious. I knew Sunny Marriner's work on the ridiculous number of sexual assaults that the Ottawa police were deeming "unfounded." I had read Catharine A. MacKinnon and her theory that "man fucks woman; subject verb object." I had done my homework. I knew enough to be cynical. Add on the police's complete disregard for Xavier's behaviour up to that point, and you had a very skeptical young woman telling two cops a horror story while dressed like a fifth-grader.

The male officer walked through every room of my apartment, while the female officer asked me to take a seat wherever I felt most comfortable. I remember watching her gunmetal grey clipboard and staring at the freckles on her hand as she pulled out a few sheets of paper. "Start from the beginning," she instructed, "but only give me the big stuff. Save the details for the written statement."

I was nervous and could tell I was doing a poor job of covering it up. I spoke a mile a minute, giving her the gist in one long stream. She asked to see the "documents" I had mentioned in my overview, and I went into my bedroom to retrieve the pile I had prepared for their arrival with all of Xavier's notes and emails stacked neatly in chronological order. She handed me one of the pages she was holding and told me to write out the story from the beginning, imploring me to go into as much detail as possible. Dates, times, witnesses. "Don't worry about running out of room. I have as many pages as you need."

She scanned the evidence I handed her. My cheeks burned scarlet as she went over every humiliating note and message. The sexually explicit emails. The cheesy love poems. I kept my head down, avoided eye contact, and wrote. The male officer sat in the living room, looking out the window.

I wrote and wrote and wrote. It must have taken me at least thirty minutes to get it all down. I went on autopilot and treated the statement like an assignment about someone else's life. I was methodical and detailed, and wrote out every painful moment of my life post-Xavier with a detachment I had mastered.

When I was done, she scanned my statement and tucked it away into her metallic clipboard. They said a detective would be assigned to my case, and in the interim, I was to stay in constant contact with trusted people in my life. "Call when you leave the house, call when you arrive at your destination. Never go longer than a few hours without connecting with someone," she told me, ignoring that this was an era in which cell phone calls were expensive and texts cost twenty-five cents each. Not to mention how much of a burden that placed on my friends and family.

But I didn't protest. I simply nodded and promised to do as I was told. Before leaving, the officers informed me that I would be contacted by a Victim/Witness Assistance Program representative. VWAP is a government program, funded by the Ministry of the Attorney General, that offers free support to victims and witnesses of crimes who are involved in the legal system in some way. In particular, they told me that it was likely that a VWAP rep would want to come by and do a safety audit of my apartment.

A day or two later, I welcomed another two clipboard-wielding strangers into my apartment. The older woman took the lead, while her tiny younger intern quietly followed behind her. I was polite but uncomfortable. I never got used to the invasions of my privacy. As they scanned my apartment, checking out every nook and cranny, the seriousness of my situation sunk in. They cased the place through Xavier's eyes, trying to expose every weakness in my plan to stay safe.

We took a seat on the couch, while the leader explained the process to me. They would do a detailed scan of my apartment and then leave me with a written plan to follow as I awaited further instructions from police. As she spoke, my phone rang.

I let it ring until the answering machine clicked on. "Hi, you've reached Sandra and Julie," the message went, and her eyes widened.

"You have to change that! You can't put your name on your answering machine! My God!"

I stammered something about how Sandra and I were both looking for new jobs, so we needed our machine to be accessible if prospective employers called. She didn't care. Having my name on my answering machine was careless, she insisted. Which baffled me because my file had clearly outlined that Xavier knew where I lived and *called my house dozens of times a day.* He already had the number! But I took the scolding quietly and could feel myself drifting away. The anxiety of having strangers in my house was one thing, but their dismissive tone made me shut down.

She proceeded to the sliding door and stepped onto the balcony. With a wave of a hand, she told me not to worry about that door because I lived on the seventh floor "and it's not like he can climb up." I clearly had more confidence in Xavier's determination than she did, but I didn't protest. I just nodded and continued to follow her around the apartment.

She checked the locks on the main door and was satisfied that my deadbolt and chain were sufficient. "Your bathroom is the only other door that locks from inside, so if he breaks in, grab your phone, lock yourself in the bathroom, and call 911." Her words indicated that the situation was serious, but her tone of voice and body language gave her away. She didn't give a fuck. She was just doing her job, and it was clear that she was following a script, going through a routine, and didn't really think she was facing down someone whose life was in danger.

This was confirmed when she went to leave. As she stood at the doorway, intern in tow, writing down some final notes, she looked up at me and asked, "How old is Xavier anyway?"

I assumed she was asking for her file, so I gave her his date of birth. "He's nineteen? Oh my God. He's *such a baby!*"

. . .

WITH AN OFFICIAL POLICE STATEMENT AND A SAFETY plan in place, my next step was to get a peace bond. Although the 911 operator had been kind enough to tell me about peace bonds, I was so taken aback that I never thought to ask about the details. Ever the keener, I didn't like to be unprepared, so I emailed a few of my women's studies professors to see if they had any resources for me. One of them suggested the University of Ottawa's Community Legal Clinic. "They offer free legal advice and specialize in violence against women, so they should have what you need." She was right.

On a sunny afternoon, I leaned against the kitchen counter and called the clinic. I briefly explained my situation and was transferred to a soft-spoken woman who proceeded to walk me through the peace bond process, step by step. First, I was to go to the Ottawa courthouse downtown, find the reception desk, and inform them I was looking for a peace bond. Then I would be taken to a small office where I would need to swear on a Bible that I was telling the truth and proceed to detail all the things Xavier had done that would warrant the peace bond. Then I would be given a date and would need to appear in court to hear the decision from a panel of justices. If it was approved, then Xavier would need to stay a certain distance away from me for one year.

It sounded intimidating but doable. Thinking I had everything I needed, I thanked her for the help, but she cut me off to inform me that Xavier would be present at the court date and that both of us were entitled to bring legal representation. I froze. The image of him and me together in court made me panic. But the thought of him being there *with a lawyer* turned my stomach to liquid. I had to sit down for fear I was going to pass out or puke.

Xavier's family had more money than mine, and so far, his family had been supporting him. His sister had even called me at one point, with a sobbing Xavier in the background, begging me to give him another chance because he was so devastated by the breakup. If he was entitled to a lawyer, there was no doubt he would get one.

I wasn't so lucky. I was a broke student desperately trying to shield my family from how bad things were getting. As I explained all this to the lovely lady from the legal clinic, she gave me a glimmer of hope by suggesting I apply for a legal aid lawyer. It turned out the legal system saw poor people all the time, so there was a government-funded program for accessing a lawyer. It meant one more hoop, but there was no way I was going to let Xavier outnumber me in a courtroom.

It was late August 2005 and Ottawa's summer heat raged on. My friend Kristen had agreed to come to the courthouse with me. I put on my fanciest work clothes and approached the reception desk. They handed me a single-page document and told me to fill it out to the best of my abilities while I waited to be called in. Kristen and I huddled together in the waiting area and wrote out my birth date and address and Xavier's contact information. It asked for a date range of the incidents and left a small space to briefly describe "what happened to make you fear for your safety." My massive, child-like handwriting spilled over the lines, as I outlined a month's worth of terror in big bubble letters.

My name was called, and I left Kristen in the waiting room. I entered a small office, where a tiny woman sat across from me. In a detached, business-like tone, she asked me to raise my left hand and solemnly swear that I would tell the truth. *This is some* Law and Order *shit,* I thought as I placed my hand on a Bible and acknowledged that I understood the legal ramifications of lying.

She input my contact information into her computer and then read over my paragraph of reasons why I was afraid, making notes and grammatical corrections. I thought it was a weird time to give a shit about verb tenses, but I sat stiffly in my chair, not giving myself away. She informed me that my court date was September 16. I was to present myself to the courthouse for 8:30 a.m., but it might take hours before I was called to the bench. I was to bring with me any documents that I thought were pertinent. She handed me back the form and dismissed me from the room.

I did as the police had instructed me to and kept in constant contact with friends whenever I left the house. It got to be a running joke among my friends, where I would call them from my apartment to tell them what I was eating or watching on TV. "Just having some lasagna. Thought you should know! Pertinent detail, I'm sure!"

My life felt so damn dramatic, and to hide my humiliation, I joked about it as much as possible. I just wanted a normal life. If I couldn't have one, I was determined to be as flippant as possible in order to avoid sitting with the reality that my life was in danger. Laughing at the absurdity of the situation was my way of regaining some control. If I joked about it, I made others feel better, and instead of them worrying about me, we could laugh together at how fucking stupid it all was. "This is nuts, right?"

I knew humour wouldn't fly with the cops, so I treated the whole legal process like a school assignment. Step one, police report. Step two, peace bond application. Next step, securing a legal aid lawyer.

I asked my friend Laura to switch shifts with me so I could go to the Legal Aid Ontario office first thing when it opened. Heading to the nondescript downtown building, I sweated through my dress clothes as I circled the streets, trying to find a parking spot. I walked into the office five minutes after opening time, and the waiting room was already packed. Grabbing a number, I took the last seat and reviewed my documents. I had filled out all the paperwork online and meticulously organized my documents to prove that not only was I incredibly broke and deserving of legal assistance but I was also dealing with a serious case of harassment that required legal intervention. I was so nervous and the waiting was sheer agony.

Finally, my number was called. I entered a small office with what appeared to be the most bored person on the face of the planet. I nervously handed over my documents and way-too-quickly rushed through my story and why I was there.

She scanned my pages as I spoke. "So, to be clear, you're not being accused of a crime?" she asked me.

Stunned, I explained that I had done nothing wrong. *Xavier* had. I was here to get a lawyer to ensure I was protected during the peace bond process.

She took my documents, reorgaznized them. and then handed them back to me. "Legal aid is for those who are being accused of a crime. You're not a defendant. You're a complainant. You have a choice in this; he doesn't. So you are not entitled to legal aid. If he needed it, he could get it. But you're not eligible for any assistance."

I felt tears well up and bit the inside of my cheek. *I am not giving this fucking paper pusher the satisfaction of seeing me cry,* I thought. Instead, I gave her a curt "Thank you" and stormed out of the office, catching my breath only when I hit the sidewalk. I hugged the neatly organized evidence that I was deserving of help, and cried behind my sunglasses on the way to my car.

Since I had paid for a full day of parking but only ended up needing a few hours, I tried my luck with the parking attendant. I was so broke that I had spent a half day trying to convince the government to get me a lawyer. I needed that damn parking refund, but the attendant didn't care. He handed me back my keys and went back to watching his mini-TV, ignoring me.

I drove to my shitty job at the mall, numb from the confirmation that no one gave a rat's ass about me. I was alone.

As I crossed the threshold of our store, my friend piped up, "Hey! How'd it go?" naively optimistic that the system had actually done its job. I had cried. I had gone numb. Now, I was angry. I unleashed on Laura about the stupidity of the whole process.

"Why isn't it written in bold letters on the legal aid website that you're only eligible if you're the fucking sketchbag? I wouldn't have waited in line at the bank to get proof of how broke I was, filled out all the damn legal aid paperwork, paid for parking, *then* waited in damn line for a half day if I knew I wasn't eligible!" I kept my voice down so customers wouldn't suspect, but my face was flushed and I was raving.

Laura routinely passed the time at work by drawing these hysterical comics that mocked the absurdity of retail life. Think the irreverence of *The Office* meets *Cathy* comics. Long before social media, she would draw them out by hand in pencil and paste them in the back room as a welcome whenever we started a new shift. I still have a comic from that day, where Laura detailed my horrific day of being screwed by legal aid and the parking attendant. Except in her version, I had a pet grizzly bear who came and ate everyone who wronged me that day, including Xavier.

Crestfallen from my legal aid debacle, I returned to numbness. I routinely joked that my highs and lows were my classic Gemini traits. I was twenty. I didn't know a damn thing about physiological responses to trauma. I didn't yet know about the neurobiology of trauma or the "window of tolerance" and the way traumatic experiences jostle our brain's ability to function properly. A term introduced by psychiatrist Daniel J. Siegel, the window of tolerance is your brain's comfort zone. Not too stimulated, not too tired, it's the optimal range of arousal for each person to live their best life. If you get too stimulated, your brain loses the ability to keep it together and you drop from intense hyperactivity to flatlining.

But I knew none of this then and took numbness as progress because it looked better than sobbing all the time. I got up every morning. I showered. I went to work on time. Depressed people didn't do those things, I thought. As long as I continued to achieve these daily tasks, I figured I could fake it till I make it. I would role-play normalcy until it came true.

Starting my third year of university, I thought that taking an extra credit would keep me extra busy and distract me from the chaos of my life. While keeping my coursework in order, I also stared down my trial date. I was so wrapped up in accepting that I had called the cops on Xavier and that my teacher's-pet, never-been-in-trouble self was going to court that I never stopped to think about how Xavier would be served.

As helpful as the 911 operator and the lady from the Community Legal Clinic had been, no one informed me that Xavier would be served paperwork in the middle of the day, at his work, which sat in a kiosk in the middle of the mall. No one told me that Xavier would be given ten days' notice to appear in court. In our "innocent until proven guilty" legal system, Xavier was entitled to legal counsel and plenty of notice to appear.

On a practical level, this meant that a man who wouldn't leave me alone was handed a legal document while at his workplace, telling him that in ten days' time, he would be defending himself against accusations that could put restrictions on his life for up to a year. On a practical level, this meant that an angry, volatile man got the message that he had nothing left to lose. I had "gotten him into trouble" and needed to be stopped.

I hadn't done any safety planning. I hadn't thought about this ten-day period because *no one told me*.

But I quickly found out my mistake when Xavier called me, emailed me, messaged me, drove to my house, paced by my work, and made every attempt to reach me and say, "You cannot do this. I will not allow you to do this." He tried threats. He tried sweet-talking. He told me, over and over, that I was overreacting. That this was serious business. That he didn't deserve this. That if I didn't go through with it, he'd be good again. That he'd be who he used to be.

That if I went through with it, I would regret it.

I wavered like a tree in a hurricane. No part of me wanted Xavier to get into trouble. I just wanted him to stop hurting me.

I had initially thought that a peace bond would be the perfect solution because he would serve no jail time, he wouldn't be arrested, and nothing would be on his record. But he kept insisting that it would ruin his life. He spent hours convincing me that I was overreacting. "You willingly came back to the apartment so many fucking times. I didn't kidnap you. Now you're going to act like you don't want me around? You're fucking lying."

I started to doubt myself. I didn't think I was strong enough. What if I got the peace bond and then he suckered me into seeing him? I'd already pissed off so many people by continuing to talk to him. If a legal protection order was in place and *I* violated it? I'd have no one left.

And what if this piece of paper was what *really* set Xavier off? His violence thus far had been limited to rape and manipulation, two things I had survived so many times. But what if things got worse? I oscillated and no one had any patience for it.

I had tried to protect my family from the worst of it, and since they lived six hours away, it was easy to do. My brother had changed his mind about school and moved home, so with no family physically around, it was easy to control the narrative. I had told them the "good bits" that allowed me to keep up the semblance of being a good daughter who had done the right things. They knew the police had taken a statement and that I had applied for a peace bond. But as the trial date loomed, they called to check in.

I must have been feeling particularly vulnerable, because I told them I was no longer so sure about this whole restraining order business. Xavier had insisted that he would quit, so why would I need to go through all the rigmarole of a trial? I conveniently omitted the whole *What if he kills me?* part. But no matter. My parents went *off*. I was being stupid. I was being naive. I was an otherwise smart person.

Not content to guilt-trip me on their own, they put a family friend on the phone. Sally was an outspoken survivor of childhood sexual abuse who had worked with vulnerable women for years. She didn't share my parent's panicked rage, but chose instead to try and reason with me. "Xavier is a textbook bad guy. They do this all the time. They know they're about to get caught, so they try and manipulate you into taking the fall for them. But trust me—Xavier will never stop. He's dangerous and you need to do this."

I could sense her kindness and concern. I didn't want to disappoint anyone. I had kept up appearances because I didn't want people to worry. I wanted to look like I had my life together. And here I was, letting everyone down.

The stress of juggling Xavier, work, and an over-full course load was getting to me. I was exhausted all the time and losing weight rapidly. I felt like something had to give, but I needed validation that I had the right to fall apart. I decided to book an appointment with the health and counselling services on campus. I wanted to bounce my peace bond decision making off a neutral third party and discuss the pros and cons of dropping my extra course.

It was early in the school year, so I was assigned a counsellor right away. I sat in the waiting room, surrounded by coughing students who were waiting to get doctor's notes. My name was called and I walked into a sunny, brightly coloured office. The counsellor fit every stereotype of an aging therapist. Long grey hair tucked into a bun, she wore a flowy tunic on top of leggings with Birkenstocked feet. She spoke softly and asked me how I was doing.

I had never spoken to anyone about the mental impacts of Xavier's behaviour. Up until that point, it was all business. Times, dates, filling out forms. But here was a complete stranger asking me for real talk about how things were going. I started to cry immediately and told her about my indecisiveness and my fear that the stress of it all would lead me to flunk my semester.

When I finished outlining the whole tale, she handed me a tissue and told me that the first course of action was to drop a class. "Six classes is a lot for anyone, but you're in no condition to be taking that many classes right now. You won't lose your scholarship, because five classes is considered full-time. And it's early in the semester, so you'll get a full refund," she assured me.

I was instantly relieved. I was concerned about my health, but I also wanted to keep up appearances. Knowing I could still be a studious full-time student while dropping a class was a huge help. Up to that point, she had been leaning back in her chair, legs crossed, with a notebook in hand. But then she settled her notebook on the desk and leaned toward me. In a deep, serious tone, she informed me that I *absolutely* needed to go ahead with the peace bond. She repeated all the same lines I had heard from my friends, my parents, Sally. "Xavier's never going to stop. He won't stop until he kills you. He's manipulating you. Don't fall for it."

All the buoyancy I had felt moments earlier evaporated. I was devastated. There was clearly no way around it. I had to go ahead with this, or I would lose the right to be upset about Xavier.

Our time was almost up, but before dismissing me, she wanted to teach me a grounding technique. "Pick a colour," she said. Red came to mind, so she asked me to pick out five red things I could see in the room. "That book, your necklace, my notebook, that file folder, and that big textbook over there." Anytime I felt anxious, I was to pick a colour and find five things in my surroundings that fit the description. "It will distract your brain and calm your heartbeat, and what's great is that it's very subtle so you can do it on the bus or in public somewhere and no one will know." It was helpful advice I would go on to use many times.

My next appointment fell on a day when I was feeling pretty great. I told her so and she attributed it to our last session, so she asked me to write a review of Carleton's counselling services "because we're constantly dealing with funding cuts, so it helps to show that our work is helping students." Crestfallen that she seemed more interested in the review than in unpacking my situation, I lied and told her I was going to go ahead with the peace bond process. I wrote a lovely review on bright-coloured paper she handed me, thanked her, and left. I never went back.

I told Xavier I would revoke my request if he left me alone. I told my parents I wasn't going to go through with it. They didn't hide their disappointment, and I swallowed the hurt. But in my mind, I was psyching myself up to do it. *Tell him you'll revoke your request and he'll calm down and then you can do it in the courtroom and then he can't touch you. There'll be cops there. And if he does keep talking to you, you'll have this fancy piece of paper to put an end to it.*

The day of our court hearing, I put on the fanciest clothes I had. A pink collared shirt, the nicest black dress pants I owned, and these black heels I had bought with my first big paycheque. I walked outside my apartment, heading for my car, and spotted Xavier. He was in his car, waiting for me. He got out and blocked my path. He told me to get into the car, to go to that courtroom, to revoke my request, and if I did, "things will be okay." He went on, "Otherwise, if I'm going down, you're going down with me. Don't you want to come home?"

I wanted to be the type of woman who punches an asshole like that in the mouth. I wanted to be strong enough to scream at the top of my lungs. To call 911 and to watch that fucker burn.

But I was not that woman.

I was twenty years old. I was terrified, exhausted, brainwashed, and bonded to that man. So I got into the car.

We arrived at the courthouse on Friday, September 16, 2005, at 8:30 a.m. Multiple people were given the same date and timeslot, so they tell you to show up, sign in, and then sit there. We sat while lawyer after lawyer went up to a panel of justices and demanded a remand. "We don't have all the documents"; "It's a conflict with an important meeting they can't miss"; on and on it goes.

The only courtroom I had ever seen was on American crime TV shows. I sat there, trying to ground myself by connecting with the hard wooden bench, but I felt myself drift away. I sat beside my abuser and watched person after person ask for a recess or a remand or some version of it. I sat in a courtroom, beside my abuser, as a drunk man with all his belongings in a garbage bag lay asleep on the bench in front of us.

They finally called our names. I took the very long walk to the front of the courtroom and stood beside Xavier.

One of the panel members asked if we were who he had called forward. We identified ourselves. The justice then made a joke about how I looked like Xavier's lawyer because I was so well dressed, and meanwhile he had worn these tacky windbreaker-type pants. Remember those? We called them "slush pants" when I was growing up. They're hideous. He wore those, with flip-flops and a stained shirt, his hands stained with ink from his day job fixing printers. I had my pretty pink collared shirt on. And the justice made a joke about me being overdressed.

Another justice asked me to plead my case. I nervously said in a small voice I didn't recognize, "I'm here to revoke my request. I've changed my mind." I was shaking and visibly terrified.

One justice on the panel sighed loudly and declared in front of the whole courtroom, "Of course you're revoking, because you're clearly not afraid of him if you showed up to court with him." Another dramatically drew an X across a piece of paper and went on to pontificate about how I made real victims look bad. I had clearly made everything up for attention and that's why real women don't come forward, because they're afraid of looking like a liar like me. I was the reason women got abused and the justices wanted everyone in that courtroom to know it.

"We're closing this file. *Next please.*" And with that, we were dismissed.

Never in my life have I felt more humiliated. Never in my life have I been more demoralized. With those justices' words, I wanted the floor to open up and swallow me alive. I wanted the God I didn't believe in to strike me dead where I stood. I wanted to die.

The whole process had taken less than five minutes, and the only thing Xavier had to do was state his name.

I don't remember walking out of that courtroom. I don't remember walking to Xavier's car. I don't remember him driving me to work. I don't remember any of it.

But I do remember Xavier turning to me in the car and saying, "You did good, babe."

Not sure why you didn't answer the door but I'm tired of chasing you down with e-mail, etc... Could you just call me so we can get this CD pictures business over and done with. Thanks.

'Hey Beautiful!

You've been on my mind ALOT lately and I don't know why; I've been dreaming of you for the last few nights... they're actually mainly nightmares and I wake up every hour or so and just lay there.

I've kinda been seeing someone recently and maybe that has something to do with it. Snuggling with another girl seems next to impossible but I've tried it and it makes me sad.. when it should make me happy.

I'm still taking those pills but I forget to take them every so often and I'm going back to the doctor's to get more...

I loved it the other day when we were just talking aside to talking about ███████ I don't care to talk about him.

Speaking of which, I called you this morning to ask you if I could pick you up but you never came home last night again, I also kinda just wanted to hear your voice

I miss you so much as my girlfriend, or even fiancee, but I miss you even more just as my friend.. you'll never understand.

For some reason, especially today, I'm really down. I'm trying to stay positive but I keep fucking up shit at

RECOGNIZANCE TO KEEP THE PEACE
UNDER SECTION 810 OF THE CRIMINAL CODE OF CANADA
OFTEN REFERRED TO AS A "RESTRAINING ORDER" OR "PEACE BOND"

PLEASE COMPLETE THIS FORM IN ORDER TO LAY AN INFORMATION UNDER SECTION 810 OF THE CRIMINAL
CODE OF CANADA.

NAME OF INFORMANT: Julie ▓ Lalonde

ADDRESS OF INFORMANT: ▓

TELEPHONE NUMBERS: (H) ▓ (W) ▓

THE INFORMANT SAYS THAT S HE HAS REASONABLE GROUNDS TO BELIEVE THAT:

NAME OF DEFENDANT: ▓

ADDRESS OF DEFENDANT ▓

ALTERNATE ADDRESS: ▓

DATE OF BIRTH OF DEFENDANT: ▓

THE INFORMANT SAYS THAT S HE HAS REASONABLE GROUNDS TO FEAR AND DOES FEAR THAT THE

DEFENDANT WILL CAUSE PERSONAL INJURY TO _____ OR HIM/HER, OR TO

HIS/HER WIFE/HUSBAND _____ AND/OR CHILD(REN) _____

Monday, August 1st to August 23rd 2005

OR WILL DAMAGE HIS/HER/THEIR PROPERTY ON ACCOUNT OF, ON OR ABOUT THE _____ DAY OF

_____, 200__ AT THE CITY OF OTTAWA,

Please describe briefly, what happened to make you fear for your safety. If it was a verbal threat, please write
down the exact words, in quotations, that were said. For example: "I am going to kill you."

I received written notes regarding threats towards
~~myself~~ me, my vehicle. My friends and family have also ~~family~~
received harassing phone calls. The police spoke with him and
told him to stop contacting me. He continued to. He has
~~hacked~~ into my computer, and is black mailing me in order to
return my passwords. He has also harassed me at my place of work.

(margin/interlined notes: "BY WRITING" · "and harassment" · "BY TRYING TO LOCATE my THROUGH MY FRIENDS & FAMILY")

IT IS YOUR RESPONSIBILITY TO ATTEND COURT, OR HAVE SOMEONE ATTEND ON YOUR BEHALF ON

16TH DAY, THE September DAY OF _____ 2005, AT 8:30 AM IN

COURTROOM NUMBER FIVE (5) AT 161 ELGIN STREET, OTTAWA, ONTARIO AND AT EVERY ADJOURNMENT

THEREAFTER UNTIL THE MATTER IS FINISHED BEFORE THE COURTS.

INFORMANT = Person who gives information.

DEFENDANT = Person required to answer a legal action against them.

4
Requiem

CATHOLICS LOVE A GOOD FUNERAL. WE LOVE A THREE-DAY affair replete with an open casket and tiny little sandwiches the church ladies make. In my family, we hang out with our dead at the Laughlin Funeral Home. Gilded gold mirrors are hung alongside preserved butterflies and taxidermy squirrels; mismatched gold thrones in the parlour nestle between gaudy water features. There isn't an empty space to be found anywhere. It's dusty as hell and wall-to-wall stuff.

I've buried so many people, I've lost track of how many hours I've spent in that funeral home. My first funeral was for my paternal grandfather. My mother was barely twenty-five and had to cart her four- and five-year-old kids into a car and drive them across the province to bury her father. My grandfather had been sick, but he was only fifty-two, so his funeral was devastating.

We were absurdly well behaved (so my mother tells me), but my brother and I were too young to understand what was going on as we were shuttled from place to place, looking up at sobbing adults. My big brother is the most empathetic human being I've ever known and has always had my back. He tried to be protective all day, but absorbing everyone's pain proved to be too much and he spontaneously vomited all over himself. His heart couldn't take it.

Five years later, my great-grandmother's lungs gave out, and my brother and I found ourselves huddled on the floor of the ER waiting room, holding hands to keep ourselves steady. Then we nervously chugged orange juice from plastic cups at the funeral home and ate mints from the candy dishes. Our great-grandmother, our Mémère, was the life of every party and loved schooling her family at cards and stuffing us with warm apple pie. She had a pet bird and a cackle that would fill the room. We loved her very much.

My brother and I grew up surrounded by elders, so we were acutely aware of our own mortality—but it never made death any easier. You do learn to go through the motions, though. I had funeral clothes, a funeral jacket, heels I knew I could stand in for hours on end. Knowing that elders loved a receiving line, I perfected the tight smile needed to console those who came to hug you and share their condolences and wanted you to hold them as they fell apart.

I went to funerals for elders who had been sick for years, the air somber but light with gratitude that their suffering was now over. I went to the funeral of a friend who took his own life, two days after partying hard at my house. I went to the funeral of a young family friend who was murdered by her ex-boyfriend. My father took on being stoic as my mother and I huddled alongside him, stunned from shock.

On an unusually warm long weekend in May, my parents and I were driving to dinner in our fanciest clothes when we had to slam the brakes on the highway. A young man had run onto the highway in front of a semi-trailer, taking his own life. His body was splayed across the road. My father jumped out of the vehicle and sprang into action, redirecting traffic. After a panicked call to 911, I watched a construction worker pull over and lay his reflective vest across the young man's face, trying to preserve the last ounce of his dignity.

Unable to sit still, I approached the driver of the semi, who looked right through me as he repeated, "He just ran out in the road. There was nothing I could do. He just ran right in front of me." I tried to reassure him, but I knew it was pointless.

· · ·

WHEN I FELT SO ABANDONED BY THE LEGAL SYSTEM THAT I swore it off completely, it felt like a heavy door had been slammed in my face. Xavier was still on his worst behaviour, and the reality that it would never stop suffocated me. I knew my life was at risk. I knew I would never be safe. Death and I have never been strangers, but we would soon be reacquainted like old friends as I learned to live with death's shadow hanging over me.

My life was terrifying but it needed to go on. I had classes to attend, papers to write, rent to pay. Xavier's constant monitoring meant I had no safe place to land, but Sandra's erratic behaviour made everything worse. I was so wrapped up in my own chaotic life that I didn't have the wherewithal to really see what was happening, but it's clear to me now that Sandra was unwell.

She only left the house for work and the occasional errand. She literally put a groove in the couch cushion from sitting there for hours on end, mindlessly watching television. Her cat and my cat had never properly adjusted to each other, and because Sandra refused to neuter her cat, he pissed on everything. If I put something on the floor for a minute and walked away, I'd come back to it soaked.

One night, I came home from class to see that my laptop's keys were ripped out. Upon closer inspection, it was clear that Tenacity had used my laptop as a litterbox and first pissed on the thing, then clawed at the keys in an attempt to cover it up.

Sandra was apologetic but insisted she was too broke to buy me a new one.

She also had a terrifying temper. Coming home from work one sunny afternoon, I opened the apartment to see things strewn across the living room and kitchen. Panicked that Xavier had broken in, I rushed to see what had happened and found the phone ripped out of the wall, and the coffee table and its contents overturned. I saw no sign of Xavier or evidence of a break-in, so I waited for Sandra to come home. She nonchalantly informed me that a telemarketer had called her while she was trying to watch TV, and it had annoyed her so much that she'd ripped the phone out of the wall and flipped a table. She explained this to me as though it were a completely rational reaction.

Living with her felt unnecessarily stressful, but I felt like I owed her for having my back. She had taken me in and borne witness to all of Xavier's bullshit. In many ways, she was an incredible friend who'd spent countless nights validating that Xavier was the problem, that I didn't deserve any of it. She hid some of Xavier's notes around her room, lest he riffle through my room. She also knew that I was easily manipulated and that it was entirely possible that Xavier would just guilt-trip me into handing the notes back. She wasn't wrong.

The only bright light in my life was my budding relationship with James. The man in the Toys "R" Us parking lot who'd come to my rescue that night with Xavier had turned out to be a certified hottie. He'd followed up on his promise to get me a local mechanic and slyly turned it into a date. He picked me up in his '76 Beetle and took me out for a coffee. He was sweet and it felt cool to share my obscure hobby with someone my age.

In my eyes, it was purely platonic. My life was so intertwined with Xavier that the idea of dating felt laughable. Who would want to date someone with a psycho ex-boyfriend? So we did a lot of hanging out. We went to coffee shops, watched obscure movies, and spent hours talking. He never seemed freaked out by Xavier or the chaos of my life. He never made me feel like I was dramatic. He believed me. And one day, he kissed me. Shortly after, he asked me to be his girlfriend. I said yes as long as we kept it very, *very* casual. I tried to play it cool but I was elated.

I knew Xavier would be livid, but I thought as long as I kept things casual with James, Xavier would never find out. The weekend James and I officially started dating, my beloved Oma died. The brain tumour that had caused her paralysis four years earlier had come back, and it was inoperable. She was sixty-three. I took the midnight Greyhound bus home, tossing and turning the whole way. I arrived exhausted at 6 a.m. and was met with one of my dad's famous bear hugs. I was devastated.

It was back to the Laughlin Funeral Home. Back to tiny cups of orange juice and languishing for hours among dead rodents. But my grandmother had insisted on shaking things up. She'd insisted that women be among her pallbearers. As the eldest granddaughter, I helped carry her casket into the church along-side my great-aunt, who was one of the first female police officers in Canada. Oma was given a true feminist send-off.

I couldn't stay long because it was in the middle of the semester. A day after her funeral, I was back on a bus to Ottawa.

Small-town news travels fast, so Xavier heard about my Oma's death and used it as an excuse to get in touch with me. He manipulated me into seeing him again, and we agreed to meet at a coffee shop. He made some excuse to bring me back to his latest apartment. This time it was a room he was renting in a house in the suburbs. He said he had left a gift behind for me and we needed to quickly swing by to grab it. "My room-mates are there, so it'll be just a quick in and out," he insisted.

It took me all of ten seconds to realize he had lied and no one was home. I felt myself slipping away, acquiescing, and walking with him to his room. It felt like a trance. I could look down and see my legs walking, but I couldn't feel them. Somehow I ended up on the bed, and as he went to unzip my jeans, I suddenly became very alert. I don't know if it was the confidence that comes from the lust of a new relationship. I don't know if this felt like cheating on James. But suddenly, I was emboldened.

I sat up and pulled his hand away. "We don't have to bang," he softly assured me. "I just want to feel you."

He inched closer to me again and made another grab for my pants. I pushed past him to get off the bed. "What the fuck are you doing?" he snapped as he grabbed my wrist and pulled me back down. I saw something flash across his eyes as he started yelling at me. "I fucking knew you were hooking up with that fucking guy. I saw you two together and tried to be cool. I tried to give you your space."

James and I had been dating for barely two weeks. I felt so naive for thinking I could slip something past Xavier. I didn't want to confirm or deny his accusations. If I said yes, I have a boyfriend, then who knows what Xavier would do. If I denied my relationship with James, it would make me a terrible girl-friend. So instead, I sweetened my voice and deflected.

"I love you, Xavier. You know that. I'm sorry you're so sad and lonely." It wasn't the sex he was looking for, but it gave him enough attention that he softened and started tearing up. I held him as he cried about how much he missed me and how he just wanted to bring me a present and how I had ruined his night. I said I was sorry, over and over.

Maybe that night was my breaking point. Maybe I was fed up with walking on eggshells at home with Sandra. Maybe I had grown a bit stronger. But I'd reached my limit and decided to strike out on my own. I wanted to get my own place and try living alone. It would get me away from Xavier, from temperamental Sandra and her goddamn cat, and it would give me an opportunity to feel like the adult I had always wanted to be. I was broke, but I found a cute little one-bedroom apartment in a shady neighbourhood that was a quick bus ride to work and school.

Sandra responded to the news that I was moving out by ripping every picture frame off the wall and smashing it on the floor in front of me. She didn't say a word as she went into her room, ripped the computer monitor out of the wall, and threw it on the floor too. I had lent it to her, so I suppose it was her dramatic way of returning it.

Barefoot, my feet covered in blood from the broken glass, I began to verbally unleash on her with such a fury that *she* backed away from me and locked herself in her room. I hadn't gotten it all out of my system yet, so I kept yelling through the locked door. I was furious, but the truth was, it felt good to finally yell at someone. I couldn't understand why I felt so unafraid of Sandra and yet so terrified of Xavier. But as I stood there, verbally ripping into Sandra and making her cower, I felt fearless and powerful.

Once I was spent, I locked all my possessions in my room, grabbed my cat, and stayed with friends for a week until my new apartment was ready for me. A short eight months after I'd called my friends to flee Xavier in the middle of the night, I was calling on them again to help me move into a new place. The mood was decidedly lighter, and everyone was so excited for me to start fresh. I just wanted things to be different.

And for a short while, they were. I settled into my apartment and spent weeks decorating it and making it feel like home. It was a small but airy one-bedroom that had big, beautiful windows that I filled with houseplants. I put up posters, set up a little office nook in my living room, and watched movies on my tiny twelve-inch television while cuddled up with my cat on my futon.

It was a rough neighbourhood, but my neighbours were largely older immigrants who had lived in the building for decades. It was a three-storey walk-up with an unlocked front entrance and no laundry, but I turned laundry day into a fun Sunday afternoon activity. I'd cram my clothes into a laundry cart, walk the four blocks to the closest laundromat, and read books while my clothes tumbled clean. I felt like a grown woman and loved it.

As a women's studies student, I was learning about power and privilege. As a first-generation university student, who grew up working class and spoke English as a second language, I felt like a total outsider. But my professors and classmates drilled into me how privileged I was, nonetheless, and how I needed to wield that power for good. All I did all day was go to class, work, and come home. I'd spend the occasional night at James's place. I didn't go out much or party. I didn't have any real hobbies. I realized I wasn't "giving back."

So I signed up to be a mentor with Big Brothers Big Sisters. I was matched with a shy middle-schooler who was passionate about art. Once a week, I'd visit her at school and we'd hang out in an empty classroom, eat snacks, colour, and chat. She was bright, funny, and incredibly talented. She gave nothing away about how hard things were at home. I was struck by the contrast between her tough exterior and the reality of her life.

It felt good to focus on someone else's well-being and needs. It felt good to concentrate on helping. It also felt good to keep myself busy. I eventually became the mentor for a second "little," and the pace of keeping up my full course load, thirty-five hours a week of work, and volunteering didn't feel overwhelming. It felt liberating. A new apartment, no roommate drama, and a busy life left little room for my mind to wander.

Determined to keep giving back, I was inspired by a classmate to sign up as a volunteer at the local sexual assault centre. After a rigorous interview process and over sixty hours of intense training, I was a fully fledged collective member who took on monthly meetings and shifts on the support line. The training was an in-depth look at violence against women, intersectionality, and the importance of being a listening ear and facilitator for the healing of survivors.

My first shift was four hours. I spent the entire time on two intense calls with women who described the most horrific torture and abuse. I never questioned whether I was ready to hear this type of trauma. In the volunteer screening process, I had only been asked if I had accessed sexual assault support services anytime in the last year. Since I had never disclosed to anyone about Xavier's assaults and had only ever had two short sessions with a school counsellor about the peace bond process, I was not screened out.

But sitting on the phone that day, wedged into a tiny office in the sexual assault centre, I fought hard to remain present as women sobbed on the phone, recalling how sexual assault had forever changed their lives. I didn't make the direct connection to my own life. I didn't understand why my body felt numb and distant. I just fought the urge to check out and concentrated on everything I had learned about being an effective and empathetic peer educator.

The nightmares didn't start with my work to end sexual assault, but they definitely got worse. I was plagued by night terrors that ranged from straightforward rape scenes to experiences of a gory, violent death. The constant theme was that I was being hurt, and though I was screaming and yelling for help, everyone around me was an apathetic, idle bystander.

I'd wake up shaking, in a cold sweat. I'd take a hot shower and start my day. One foot in front of the other.

Although I was still getting emails and constant phone calls from Xavier and the occasional note on my car, I felt safer in my new place. I was acutely aware of his existence, but he felt like a mosquito in my ear and less of direct threat. For about a month or so.

I walked out of my kitchen one weekend, carrying a plate of food to my couch, when I swore I saw his car. Most of my apartment faced a back alley that separated my apartment building from another set of buildings. I gasped and dropped the plate, smashing it to pieces on the floor. But when I approached the window to take a second look, the car was gone. I felt so stupid. Was I getting paranoid now?

I had been living on my own about a month when I came home from work to find a note wedged under my front door. I knew it was him before I read it, and his handwriting confirmed my fears. "I will always love you, you have no choice," along with a scribbled heart, was scrawled across a piece of ripped cardboard.

At the time, the words mattered far less to me than the realization that I had, in fact, seen his car in the alley behind my house. He had found my new apartment, the one safe space I had tried to carve out for myself. I don't remember feeling afraid, concerned, or even surprised. I was annoyed. It had been nearly a year since I'd left Xavier. Deep down, I knew he would find me eventually, but I'd thought I had more time.

The sweltering Ottawa summer raged on and the only respite was keeping my windows open all night to try and let some of the cooler air in. I kept my fans running 24/7 and slept with the thinnest sheet. Sometimes, the heat would be so unbearable that I would wake up parched from dehydration. On one such occasion, I stumbled out of bed in the middle of the night to get a glass of water from the kitchen. Walking back to my room, I faced the picture windows in my living room and saw Xavier sitting in his car in the back alley. It was the middle of the night and Xavier was sitting in his car, looking up at my window, staring at me.

I don't know how long he had been there. It could have been minutes. It could have been hours. But after we locked eyes for a second, he turned his car on and sped away.

The next morning, I called a friend to install a second lock on my front door.

After that incident in the alley, the notes and gifts started to show up on my apartment's welcome mat. I'd walk up the three flights of stairs to my apartment after class, work, or volunteering and find a note or package waiting for me. Because my apartment didn't have a secure entrance, it was impossible to fully lock him out. And although I had notified my neighbours about him, no one stopped him or asked him to leave. Coming home to a bouquet of flowers leaning against my door, I had to listen to my elderly neighbour coo about the "sweet young man" she'd seen drop it off. She thought it was so beautiful that men still believed in romance. I gritted my teeth and walked inside.

Xavier was always between jobs. At one point, he held a job as a distributor of candy and chocolate bars. I've had a lifelong sweet tooth. In high school, I went so far as to paint my room in a Skittles theme, replete with a giant rainbow with the tiny colourful candies falling from it.

Coming home to my apartment after a long day of work, I found an unmarked box outside my door. I sighed, grabbed the box, and headed inside to discover that it was an entire case of candy and mini chocolate bars. Xavier had attached some note about how he just happened to be in my neighbourhood and was thinking of me. I hated that he wouldn't leave me alone, but I obviously didn't hate all the candy. I mean, I'm not a monster. If free candy was the only upside to my situation, I was going to shovel that stuff right into my face.

I never drank. I didn't do drugs. I loved to dance but hated the meat-market vibe of the bar scene. So I spent a lot of nights on my couch with friends, watching bad movies and eating junk food. I routinely hosted house parties and never outgrew my love of a good costume bash. My love of absurd themed parties rubbed off on others, and it became a running joke among my friends that we would buy each other the most random costume piece as a birthday gift.

My friend Hannah was a big fan of my weird antics, so I bought her a big plastic Viking hat. With its faux metal helmet and two giant horns, it was ridiculous. She loved it instantly.

We ended up having a major dance party at my house, and in the chaos of the 2 a.m. clean-up, she accidentally left it behind.

We made plans to hang out the weekend after. She had just gotten the full DVD set of *The Golden Girls*, so we ordered in pizza (that showed up two hours late) and settled on the couch to watch the girls do their thing. Hannah was a newer friend of mine that I had met after I'd left Xavier. She'd heard about him plenty but had never met him. But as we crushed our pizza slices and laughed at the antics of *The Golden Girls*, I spotted Xavier driving into the back alley.

I had no way of predicting how Xavier's peekaboo behaviour would affect me. Sometimes my stomach fell to the floor. Other times I would fly into a rage. Occasionally I would respond with flat-out annoyance. *Again with this shit?* I'd think. I left him a year ago, and yet, there he was.

I muted the TV and alerted Hannah to what was going on. I assured her we weren't in danger and that we could just ignore him. Looking back on it now, I can see how strange that was. "Oh, hey. Just FYI. My stalker is parked a few metres away, staring at us through the window, but chill. It's fine."

But Hannah, bless her heart, was game. She got up, grabbed her Viking hat, and proceeded to shimmy across the living room floor. She stared out the window at Xavier and mocked him through dance moves ranging from the running man to the robot and a boot scoot. After a moment of shock, I was doubled over in hysterics, laughing so hard that tears ran down my face. She looked fucking ridiculous and it was the perfect response to the absurdity of the situation. Her dance moves were epic, and the look on Xavier's face was priceless. He initially looked so confused (not that I could blame him), but once he understood what was going on, he scowled and peeled out of the alley. If I couldn't stop Xavier's crazy, I could try and match it.

The next day, he left me a note to tell me I was mean and that he was shocked to see Jackie acting in such a way and assumed I put her up to it. Since he had never met Hannah, he thought it was my demure, quiet friend Jackie, who, from a distance, looked similar to Hannah. Flying high from the experience of watching someone rub Xavier's face in it, I was unfazed by his attempts to guilt-trip me into apologizing.

A little later on, I found him walking the perimeter of my apartment building. Seeing him without the added layer of a car between us made my stomach drop. And then, not content to drive across the city to see me, Xavier moved into the apartment buildings behind my house. I processed the news the only way I knew how—by suppressing it.

The few friends I told were horrified but unsurprised. During my nightly call to James, I told him the latest development in the Xavier saga. Since I had sheltered him from the worst of Xavier's behaviour, he reacted to the news with frustration. "Why don't you just call the cops, Julie? If he's that scary, why don't you report him?" It was our first fight and it was about that fucking Xavier.

I explained to James how I had tried in vain to get the police to care. I told him that they took weeks to get back to me when I first contacted them and that after my failed attempt at a peace bond, it took weeks before an officer called to follow up. The cop called *while Xavier was in my apartment* and because he never asked if it was a good time to talk or not, I had to tell the officer, through gritted teeth, that everything was hunky dory.

James and I had started dating after I'd given up on the police, so he fell back on all the preconceptions he had of the legal system and who it was made to help. As a white man who came from a family of lawyers, he saw no reason to distrust the police. He believed that if something bad happened, they responded accordingly. Even after I explained to James the humiliation of the whole process and how I had been left to fend for myself, he insinuated that I was leading Xavier on or hadn't told the police the whole truth about what Xavier had done. He couldn't wrap his head around the idea that I was telling the whole truth, so I told him to forget about it. Again, I was alone.

I continued to go to class. I worked my thirty-five hours a week at the mall, raking in minimum wage and cramming in readings for school between customers. I worked my shifts on the support line. I slept like shit, had trouble concentrating, and routinely found myself lying in bed, staring at the ceiling for hours. But as long as I kept meeting deadlines and getting a paycheque, I chalked it up to the stresses of being a millennial in school.

Xavier's moods continued to waver. Some days he talked to me like we were old pals. Other days, if I didn't pick up the phone or wave when I saw him, he would have a tantrum and call me incessantly or leave me mountains of notes on my car and doorstep.

On a quick trip home to store my beloved Beetle at my parents' place, Xavier kept calling. Annoyed at the twelfth call, I pulled over on the side of the highway. It was dark and chilly and my car has no heat, so the cold sat in my bones. I pulled my lap blanket around me and called him back. He picked up on the first ring and didn't bother saying hello. Instead, he launched into a hysterical, sobbing rant about how he was driving erratically on the highway back in Ottawa and was going to crash his car into someone or drive off the road to his death.

"Why do you keep hurting me like this? I can't live like this. I need you and you don't care. You don't care about me. You only care about yourself," he yammered on. I could barely hear him over the sound of his sobbing. And I knew he wasn't kidding about being in the car, because I could hear the sound of the road and cars honking at him.

I shifted into support-worker mode and told him I loved him, I cared about him, and I didn't want him to die. I begged him to slow down or pull over. I threatened to hang up and call the police. I told him he was going to kill someone. Soon I was sobbing too and screaming at him to just go home. Maybe it was the knowledge that he'd gotten a reaction out of me. Maybe he was just spent. But I could hear his breathing slowing down, and after a half-hour or so, he turned the car off, safely in his parking spot at home.

My body felt like it had run a marathon. But I still had an hour or two of driving left to do, so I turned up my music, threw on my signal light, and pulled back onto the highway. When I arrived at my parents' place, I said nothing.

A week or two later, I came home to a note under my door. It was a handwritten, detailed will that explained that he was going to kill himself and make it look like an accident, but I would know the truth. Xavier was trusting me to divvy up his belongings and listed them all in painstaking detail, from his CD collection to his favourite hockey cards.

I called him repeatedly and he didn't pick up for hours. Our roles had reversed, as he'd intended, and I found myself tracking him down, worried that he would go ahead with his plan.

I wanted Xavier to leave me alone. I wanted him to give me peace and quiet. But I didn't want him to die. I didn't want him to suffer.

It was devastating to know that his heart was so broken that he would consider suicide. I hated him for putting me in that position, and although a part of me knew this was just his attempt to hurt me, I still tried desperately to walk him off the ledge.

He eventually called me back and guilt-tripped me into promising I would keep the letter safe, even though he wouldn't do anything. "I swear," he said. "But just in case."

It was always a push and pull between us. I wanted him gone, but the only way to do that was prison or death and I wanted neither of those things. Deep down, I also feared that Xavier wouldn't go down without me. I never let the reality of the threats to my life bubble to the surface. That was too scary to acknowledge. So he stayed in my orbit and I tried to carry on. I kept myself busy and took everything one day at a time.

Planning too far ahead would send me into a panic; I was horrified at the thought of Xavier still being my shadow days, months, or years into the future.

Deep in denial, I kept myself busy and buried myself in schoolwork. I upped my hours at the mall and threw myself into working full-time and taking on support line shifts. I limited how much I shared about Xavier, and unless I brought it up, no one said anything. Denial was working for everyone around me.

Through the chaos of everything, my grades had slipped in first and second year. But I'd found my academic groove again, and I had my third year behind me, having finished it with a solid GPA. That year had been a significant one for my family, too. Just as the school year was winding down, my dad had called to tell me that Papère had died. The great-grandfather who had sewed me mittens for my ski trips, and taught me card tricks and the importance of sugary desserts, had died of old age. It felt like the end of an era. I took little comfort in knowing he had lived ninety-two years. My boyfriend and friends were over for another movie night, and they helped me pull myself together to book a bus ticket home.

The next day, I worked a full shift at work, because if I wasn't working, I wasn't getting paid. James offered to come over after work to keep me company until my midnight bus ride. I packed up my trusty funeral suit and enough clothes for a few days. We settled on the couch to aimlessly watch a movie, and it turned into sex. We napped for a bit, and then it was time for me to get going. James kissed me goodbye and wished me luck.

I went to fill up my cat's food dish and do some last-minute tidying when I heard a knock on the door. I checked the peephole and saw that it was James.

"What colour is Xavier's car?" He sounded out of breath.

"It's a blue Tiburon," I said. "Why?"

"I'm not letting you leave here by yourself. Fucking Xavier's parked out front."

Xavier had gotten wind of my Papère's death. He deduced that I'd be heading home and knew the midnight bus was the only way for me to get there. In his mind, offering to drive me to the Greyhound station was the chivalrous move.

I gathered up my suitcase, gave my cat one last squish, and walked out of my building. Xavier's car was nowhere in sight, but that offered no comfort. James and I walked the two blocks to the city bus stop and waited five minutes in silence. When the city bus arrived, he kissed me and waved me onto the bus. I put my headphones on, kept my head down, and let the bus carry me to the Greyhound station.

Twenty minutes later, as I stepped off the city bus, I spotted Xavier out of the corner of my right eye. He was crossing the parking lot, walking toward me. I pretended not to notice and sped up, beelining it for the women's washroom. Once inside, I locked myself in a stall and, with shaking hands, called James.

"He's here. Oh my God, Xavier's here," I spluttered.

In the calm, deep voice that I loved so much, he responded, "Yes, I know. I'm here too."

Unbeknownst to me, Xavier and James had gotten into a screaming match once I'd hopped onto the city bus. Xavier had been watching us from a distance, and when James spotted him, he yelled at him to leave me the hell alone. "I know what you're trying to do, asshole, and you're not going to get away with it. Fuck off!"

Xavier rolled down his window and told him it was none of his business and no one could stop him, least of all a dude standing on a street corner waiting for the bus. And then Xavier sped off.

James suspected Xavier was on his way to the Greyhound station, so he called up his roommates and asked them to come meet him right away, no questions asked. They came to get him and James gave them the scoop as they sped off to the Greyhound station. They didn't have much of a plan. They just knew Xavier was coming for me and had to be stopped.

As James told me all this, Xavier suddenly burst into the women's washroom and started banging on my stall. I could hear the woman in the stall next to me freaking out while this strange man banged on the door, demanding I get out. Suddenly Xavier yelped as he was pulled out of the bathroom by the scruff of his shirt. Aaron and Martin, two of James's roommates, had dragged Xavier out of the washroom and shoved him against the wall.

Aaron was a mixed martial artist and a gym rat who I later found out was high on shrooms when he got the call from James to help out. Martin, a big, good-looking guy, stood quietly beside Aaron, making them an intimidating pair. I was still locked in my stall so I couldn't see what was going on, but I could hear the scuffle. James stayed hidden around the corner, since Xavier knew who he was. He figured Xavier would be way more freaked out if he thought two complete strangers were coming for him. He wasn't wrong.

It could have been five minutes or fifteen, but it felt like a lifetime. I called James and told him to call off the dogs. I wanted to try and reason with Xavier, and even if it didn't work, I had to get out of the bathroom. I had a bus to catch.

Aaron and Martin gave Xavier one last shove and then walked around the corner, allowing me to come out of the washroom. As soon as I saw him, I knew he was terrified but trying to play it cool.

"Who the fuck was that!" he yelled at me.

I begged him to lower his voice. The theatrics of the whole thing was humiliating. A Greyhound station is already known as a gathering place of riff-raff, and here I was, having a public fight with my "boyfriend." I also feared someone would call security. The sight of two men roughing up a smaller guy pinned against the wall wasn't going to play out well for me.

In a stern voice, barely above a whisper, Xavier scolded me for being a drama queen who showed up with a pack of wolves when he was just trying to be nice and offer me some comfort before I went home to bury an elder. "I'm just trying to be nice and as per fucking usual, you're blowing everything out of proportion. Look, I could fucking kill you *right now* and your lame bodyguards wouldn't be able to do a fucking thing. You hear me? Do you fucking hear me?"

I wanted to go toe-to-toe with him. The adrenaline of the whole situation had my heart racing. I could have punched him out right where he stood and not felt a thing. But I was also mortified. I wanted it all to end.

So I acquiesced. As always.

I told him that he needed to leave. I told him I needed to get on the bus and go home. I told him I'd forget everything and never bring it up again if he just left.

He softened and became sympathetic Xavier, concerned about me and wanting me to know he cared. The same man who had threatened my life moments before was suddenly the only person who really cared about me.

"Go, Xavier. Just fucking go," I whispered over and over as he tried to hug me.

Finally, he turned to leave and made a show of the whole thing, to ensure everyone knew he was leaving because *he* wanted to.

He rounded the corner and saw Aaron and Martin standing there, waiting for him. He put on his tough guy mask and threw his hands up, speed-walking out to his car. "I'm leaving. I'm leaving. Don't fucking touch me again. I'm leaving."

Aaron walked up behind him and yelled at him, "Yeah, you better fucking leave. And stay gone, motherfucker. You're done."

Xavier's voice shook, but he tried to play it cool as he slipped into his car and turned the key. Aaron punched the side mirror for good measure as Xavier sped off.

Meanwhile, inside the station, I went to wait in line for my midnight bus ride home. I was humiliated and desperately trying to avoid the eyes of the witnesses who had seen the whole situation unfold. I didn't want to imagine what they thought of me. It was all too much.

James came back inside and joined me in line, slipping his arms around me and whispering into my neck, "Are you okay?" I told him I was, because what was the alternative? Xavier was always going to do whatever he wanted, and all I could do is handle how I reacted to it. And in that moment, all I cared about was my exhaustion, the six-hour bus ride ahead, and the upcoming three days of Catholic funeral rites.

The bus pulled into the station and I told James to thank his friends for coming to rescue me. I was so sorry it needed to be done but was truly grateful that men I barely knew had shown up on such short notice to pull Xavier off of me. It was humiliating to have my dirty laundry aired for them to see, but it also felt incredibly validating to have two complete strangers believe me.

Never again would James question why I didn't involve police. Never again would James downplay Xavier's behaviour.

I boarded the bus, leaned my head against the glass, and tried my best to let my exhaustion overtake me. When I arrived, bleary-eyed at six the next morning, I told no one what had happened.

Julie, your phone's off the hook, was down the road after getting fired from my BS telemarketing job and came by to give you a lift. Apparently you're already gone so, hope you had fun and whatnot...

Aurevoir!

For lust and all you did was dance,
I was more hurt than ever,
And you thought you were so clever.
Doing things behind my back,
When you thought I was all whacked,
You thought you'd get away with it,
That's when I just about quit.

I never left you, I loved you too much,
You were my love, you were my life,
You are my everything…
And were soon to be my wife…

I want to thank you for all the things you have done for me,
All the things you've taught me,
I want to say fuck you, for all the mean things you've said and done,
For all the things you rub in my face,
And I want to say I'm sorry, for all the hurtful things I've done,
And all the mean things I've said.

I wish I could go back a year,
And fix all of these problems,
I just want you to hear,
That the only one I want to be with is you.

There's no chance for that to happen,
There's nothing else left for me in this world,
I don't eat, and I don't sleep,
I feel sick and lonely.

I love you. Make me proud. I'll be watching.

— Sell car and pay loan
— pay visa + master card

HG - M ins..

≈ $4000 - 3800 remaining + this weeks pay
⇒ ≈ 4500 - 400   ≈ 500

— bed, dressers, desks, furniture, lamps, etc → home
— TV, VCR, DVD, Xbox → Remi

passwords:

If you've opened this, it's either because I'm out partying in a world with no pains or you didn't listen to me. If that is the case, don't go any further as it isn't necessary. I either haven't chosen the day or decided to get back on my feet. Tell noone. You weren't supposed to open it! I'm not doing this for attention, I've just decided that my time has come. I've almost done it twice, but this one will be "accidental. Everyone wins. If all goes as planned, my last words will be with you, then I will go play hockey on the canal, then work on my car. Good way to move on, 3 things I love. Don't show this to anyone... I bought you a shredder. Use it. You found nothing more but the letter to my loved ones with nothing much on it. I left you a little something even though you wouldn't do the same for me. Live your life twice as hard as you do, life will always be too short.

♡ Always,

5
KFC and Nancy Grace

MY FAMILY HAS A WAY WITH WORDS. WITH A FRANCOPHONE mother and an anglophone father, we've perfected the art of Frenglish.

Some of my extended family only spoke French and would flex what few bilingual muscles they had only in my dad's presence. One particularly hilarious moment occurred when my younger cousin was cold and asked my dad, "Come blanket me," and then, while getting ready to leave our house, said, "I'm s'en va at my chez nous now."

My godson also tried to practise his English by asking my brother to come play hide-and-seek. Except it came out as "Come cacher with me."

I learned to read English before I could speak it, so my mother always joked about how I put my syllables in the wrong places. I mispronounced words so often that my family adopted my messy pronunciations, and I still sometimes pause to ensure I'm pronouncing oregano, basil, and Barbados properly.

My mother coached my baseball team when I was a kid. We were big fans of cheers, and mom would lead us into chants to keep up morale. At one of our earliest games, we were getting creamed. My mom tried to build us back up as we ran onto the field with a round of "Three up! Three down!" Except our team was basically a dozen ragtag twelve-year-olds who spoke in broken English, and so our attempt at "Three up! Three down!" came out as "Trees up! Trees down!" I mean, it made sense to us. Who cares if the Anglo kids from the opposing team were so confused? The chant stuck and we began adding a "zooom!" chainsaw sound to the end of it to really punch it up.

Besides our mishmash of English and French, my family also spoke in streams of quirky expressions, made-up words, and questionable labels. I grew up surrounded by adults doing voice impressions and singing songs instead of speaking. My beautiful family is loud and creative, and it was always normal to me.

My favourite lunch growing up was a tuna sandwich. My mom would always sing "Tuna, tuna! Tuna, tunaaa!" as she prepared it. I was a grown woman before I learned that the orange-coloured salad dressing I loved so much was actually called "French" and not "Frog." My mother and I share few physical characteristics other than a broad forehead and cleft chin. Having a big forehead in my family was referred to as a "MoFoDy," which means having more forehead than body.

One uncle in particular insisted on speaking in idioms, even though he could never remember them properly. So he'd respond to being ignored with "What am I? Chopped beef?" On one trip to visit us, he forgot to pack enough underwear, so he warned everyone one morning that he was going "Dakota." If his tax bill was too high, he'd complain about the government constantly demanding that he give them money, "hand over foot." Bless his heart for trying, I suppose.

My people also love a good nickname. I was Jewel for most of my life, which is pretty straightforward. My friends, however, included Lurch, Dane-Dane, Giggler, Chi-Chi, and Half-Pint.

When Xavier and I got together, we discovered a shared affinity for creative use of Frenglish. Anglophones who hung out with us referred to it as "watching satellite TV in a storm. We're with you and then it cuts out and then moments later, we're back again."

On one of our first grocery shopping trips as a newly domesticated couple, Xavier asked me to grab him some "war cheese." Confused, I asked him to come to the cheese aisle with me to point out what he meant. Turns out, marble cheese looks a lot like camouflage, so he'd started calling it "war cheese" to the point of actually forgetting its real name.

After I left Xavier, the very sound of his name would make my stomach drop. I would try so hard to keep up the facade of being indifferent to his bullshit, but his name would draw me right back. So like a true Lalonde, I decided to give him a nickname.

Xavier was no longer Xavier. He became Dickwad.

. . .

AS THE WEEKS AND MONTHS STRETCHED ON AFTER I LEFT Xavier and he still wouldn't leave me alone, calling him Dickwad gave me a small sense of distance. He wasn't really a person. He wasn't really a threat to me. He was a caricature. And since so few people knew about him or what I was going through, it was easier to pretend it was all make-believe. Dickwad became my secret, and I was really good at keeping those.

But I was approaching the end of my degree and had to figure out my next move. As a first-generation university graduate,

I thankfully didn't have any pressure from my family to continue my studies. I was already making them proud. But I had a love for school and for qualitative research in particular. At the same time, I also had real frustrations with academia and the elitist nature of the ivory tower. I was always made to feel like an outsider, which exacerbated my imposter syndrome. Add in years of living with a man who constantly took jabs at me, and I felt like a fraud. But I also wanted to do my family justice.

In my four years of pursuing women's studies and Canadian studies, I hadn't done a single reading or attended a single lecture on elderly women. It was astounding. We talked about poverty, violence, and discrimination—but only involving young women. Having grown up in a multigenerational home, I found myself constantly looking for my grandmothers' experience. Where were the stories of elderly women? Where were the stories about elderly women struggling? Both my paternal and maternal grandmothers had lived in poverty. Elderly women are one of the poorest demographics in Canada. But you wouldn't know it from what I'd studied.

I decided to apply to graduate school. I didn't have the confidence to put much effort into the application. Assuming I'd never get in, I only applied to Carleton. I figured if I didn't get in, then it would hurt less, since it wasn't like I was planning to move across the country or something.

I was excited to continue school, but mostly, I was terrified of what my mind would do if I wasn't busy. School, work, and volunteering had kept me busy enough to keep Xavier at bay. He was easier to ignore when I had so many other things on the brain. The thought of just working nine to five and having empty evenings and weekends petrified me.

My acceptance letter into graduate school at Carleton solved all my problems. My family was so proud of me, my fragile self-esteem was bolstered, and my fears of too much free time were assuaged. But first, I needed to move.

Having Xavier live behind my house was hell, and since my landlord refused to do routine maintenance, my apartment building was falling apart. The neighbourhood was unsafe, with more and more muggings and break-ins. The few people who knew about Xavier and my situation were getting vocal about how badly I needed to move. James, in particular, was adamant that I needed to get the fuck out of there. The incident at the Greyhound station had really shaken him up, and the idea that I was living alone with Xavier staring into my apartment every day drove him crazy.

I loved my little apartment. It was the first place that was truly *mine*, and I loved everything about living alone. A lifelong clean freak, I loved having everything neat and tidy. I loved coming home every day to my cat and not having to live around someone else's schedule or habits. It was the closest I had come to creating a warm place to land. Xavier was always watching, but he had never crossed the threshold into the actual apartment. If I closed all the curtains, shut the windows, unplugged the phone, and lay in the bath, I could steal a few moments for myself in all the chaos. I could pretend nothing existed outside those four walls. I didn't want to give it up.

But James presented me with an offer that was too good to pass up. He was buying a house on the outskirts of the city and wanted me to move in with him.

It had been years since I'd left Xavier. James and I had a well-established relationship. I didn't want to live with anyone, especially someone I was dating. But it was a safe neighbourhood and maybe, *just maybe*, someplace Xavier couldn't find me. James promised to only charge me rent I could afford. He also promised to punch Xavier in the mouth if he ever showed up at our door. I was in.

My cat loved having three whole floors to roam, and I had to admit that the perks of living in a house were great. Laundry. A driveway. Room for guests to sleep over!

But James quickly discovered that I was a difficult roommate. The smallest thing could trigger me and I would lie in bed, catatonic. He would think it was his fault, and I had no real awareness of what was happening, so I couldn't even explain myself. My trauma was the constant elephant in the room.

The first time he accidentally startled me, I let out the most blood-curdling scream and collapsed on the floor. I was inconsolable. The second time, I threw a plate at him. We had to develop a system where he would clap his hands before he entered a room I was in until I hollered "I hear you," so he could enter without incident. And that was only the daytime quirks.

At night, I routinely flailed, muttered to myself, or started crying, all while completely asleep. If I wasn't thrashing around the bed, I was curled into a ball so tight that I routinely woke up with excruciating kinks in my neck. But we never talked about it. He just patiently endured it all while I drowned in my shame.

Xavier slowly became quiet after I moved. I still got the occasional email or phone call, but I stopped seeing him in person. He knew I'd moved, but if he figured out where my new house was, he never let on. I'd finally gotten my first real job as a teaching assistant and was able to quit selling shoes at the mall. I spent most of my time on campus and stopped seeing him around. I thought maybe Xavier had finally moved on.

I heard through our small town's grapevine that he had moved away from Ottawa. I heard conflicting stories about where exactly he'd ended up, but he was definitely out of my city. There was even a rumour that he was dating someone new.

Friends asked me how I felt about the new woman in his life, but I felt nothing. I leaned on my peer support training. I had supported enough survivors to know that what an abuser does after he's harmed you is not your responsibility. When women insisted, "I have to report him or else he'll do something to someone else and it'll be my fault!" it was my job to remind them that we are not responsible for the actions of the men who hurt us.

I had internalized very little of the training I'd received, but for some reason, that one sank in right away. I wished Xavier's rumoured new girlfriend well but never thought about contacting her. I thought that notifying her would aggravate Xavier, and I was finally enjoying some moments of quiet after all these years. And besides, what if she didn't believe me? Xavier was incredibly charming and he could easily frame me as the "crazy ex-girlfriend."

A quiet Xavier was a double-edged sword. It was unbelievable to be able to move through the world without him monitoring my every move. But on the other hand, how did I know he wasn't watching me? I remembered everything young moms had taught me about living with a toddler. The kids never stop moving and mothers pray for a moment of quiet. But then, when they go silent, you panic. *What are they up to?*

And sure enough, whenever I'd think, *He's done. He's over me. He's moved on,* I would get a message from him and spiral. Not wanting to worry others, I would make a throwaway comment to James or Taylor about that "fucking Dickwad" and punctuate it with an eye roll. And that was it.

As always, I relied on my trusty coping mechanisms of denial and a busy schedule. Other than my terrible sleep and debilitating migraines, I convinced myself (and everyone around me) that I was thriving. Besides, I spent hours supporting survivors of sexual violence who were doing way worse than me. They were struggling with substance misuse, depressive episodes, public panic attacks, and addictions to everything from gambling to online shopping. Compared to them, I was fine.

I was working fifteen hours a week as a teaching assistant, had scored a part-time job pushing paper for the federal government, was doing a full course load, and was volunteering at the local sexual assault centre. I was also trying to get a sexual assault centre started up on my campus.

The week that I started graduate school, a man broke into a lab on Carleton's campus and brutally sexually assaulted and beat a science student. The incident exposed all the gaps in Carleton's policies regarding sexual assault and sent a wave of panic through the campus community. At the time, I was a teaching assistant alongside a woman from the University of Alberta, a campus with its own sexual assault centre. She was aghast to hear that Carleton didn't even have an office of sexual assault services, let alone a centre like U of A's. Since Carleton was the only campus I had ever known, I was shocked that campus-based sexual assault services even existed. We started a lobby group called the Coalition for a Carleton Sexual Assault Centre.

The intense lobbying and advocacy work was enough to fill a full-time job. On top of grad studies, volunteering at the sexual assault centre, and two paid jobs, I was drowning. But busy was all I knew. Busy was key to keeping it together.

I had no social life and developed stomach problems, but I thought I was living my best life. Xavier lived in another city and only contacted me periodically. Sometimes I went a month or two without hearing from him. And I loved school—grad school in particular. The idea of doing my own research on a topic of my choosing made my nerdy heart burst.

My research goal was to explore the reality of being an elderly woman living in poverty and to do a rural-versus-urban comparison. I was going to do fifteen to twenty qualitative consultations with elderly woman using a semi-structured interview style. I wanted to really tell their stories and shake up traditional, boring academic writing. I had a very bumpy road ahead.

In a research methods course, a classmate was presenting her research on violence against women and the legal system's response. She played a short clip of a US judge berating a woman who was sobbing. That's all I remember about the clip. The second the judge started laying into her, I was flooded with anxiety. I felt like I was crawling out of my skin and couldn't catch my breath. I had no idea what was happening to me, but I needed to get *the fuck out* of that classroom.

This was 2007, long before the debates on trigger warnings spread across academia. I had no forewarning. She just launched right into it. And I had no awareness of what was happening to me. I didn't even make a connection between my reaction and the content of the clip. I just knew I wanted to flee. But because the class had only six people in it, I didn't want to draw any attention to myself. So I concentrated on dissociating. I told myself to just sit still and drift. I don't even remember how I got home.

I had liked my research methods course because I liked the nitty-gritty of research. I wasn't interested in theory and high-level discussions. I wanted to know the nuts and bolts of gender and how it affected our lives. So I dreaded all my theory courses and generally struggled through the coursework. I spent half a class fighting with a classmate who was offended that I would critique Judith Butler's impenetrable writing style. My classmate thought Butler had the right to be as inaccessible as she wanted. I thought her work was brilliant but she was a pompous ass. The professor sat back and enjoyed the exchange.

In fact, I scoffed through most of the content until we got to Michel Foucault and *Discipline and Punish*. The French philosopher wrote a seminal text on prison systems that explored surveillance and torture and introduced the concept of panopticism. It's complicated theoretical writing but the gist of it is a circular prison where each of the cells faces a central tower. In the tower, a bright light shines into every cell, so the people in the tower can see the cells but the people in the cell can't see out or see the other cells. The prisoners are told that there are guards within the tower at all times, but they have no way of knowing if and when they are being watched. So the prisoners act as though they are being watched at all times. The result is self-policing. The prisoners act as though they are being watched, and in doing so, remove the need for any guards to be on duty.

Foucault's theory instantly made sense to me. It was a brilliant look at surveillance and discipline, but it also felt like the most apt description of stalking.

People could tell me Xavier wasn't watching me, but it wouldn't change what my heart rate told me. I could have found myself in a locked closet with no window where I'd be able to objectively see that Xavier wasn't watching me. But I still would have felt deep panic. I felt like he was always there, always keeping tabs on me. It felt like *The Truman Show*, and no reassurance in the world did anything to change that feeling. So it felt safer to just assume he was always looking over my shoulder and to act accordingly.

Everything I said, I assumed he would overhear. Everything I wrote, I assumed he would read. I censored my speech and limited my movements without even being conscious of it. I was just always "on," and no assurance from others that he was nowhere to be found could change how I felt.

Learning about Foucault was one of the few times that I was conscious of the ways Xavier had affected my life. I was grateful to the philosopher for giving me imagery to help me understand what I was feeling. Foucault's philosophy didn't make my life any easier but it helped me ace my theory class— which allowed me to move on to the meat of doing my thesis research.

The week after I got ethics approval to begin interviews for my thesis, Ottawa bus drivers went on strike for fifty-six days. It was the middle of winter. Living on the outskirts of the city with my car in storage for the winter, I had to use half my grant money to buy another car. Not that it mattered, because the lack of transit options kept elderly women largely stuck inside, so recruitment proved to be a total nightmare. I felt cursed. I just couldn't catch a damn break.

It took me eight months to find my participants. Eventually, I found eighteen women who were willing to talk to me. One of them was Lorraine.

Lorraine lived in subsidized housing in downtown Ottawa. She was in her early seventies and had a series of health problems that made her housebound. I met Lorraine through a local service called Aging in Place, which worked to help elders live independently. The Aging in Place co-ordinator told me Lorraine was a perfect candidate "and she's a talker, so she'll love this."

I arrived to each interview the same way. I'd meet the women at their place at a scheduled time with a bouquet of flowers and a small card as a gift. After some brief introductions, we'd set up camp somewhere they felt comfortable, I would turn on the recorder, and we'd begin. Most interviews lasted somewhere between thirty minutes and two hours, depending on the subject's level of comfort and personality. My interview with Lorraine lasted nearly four hours.

She told me about her abusive marriage, her son's suicide, the pain of being trapped inside her house with a broken body but an engaged mind. Lorraine was funny, smart, and brutally honest. After the interview was over, I gave her the same spiel I'd given all the others. "Thank you so much for your generosity. My research would not exist without you. When it's done, you are welcome to a transcript of your interview. If you think of anything else you'd like to add once I'm done, here is my number. I'm happy to come by again or to chat with you over the phone." Lorraine gave me a big hug and thanked me for coming.

A few days later, she called to say she had written down some thoughts to be included, if I was still interested. When I came by to grab what I assumed would be a scrap of paper, it turned out to be a solid five pages of handwritten notes. Considering Lorraine had lost most of her eyesight and had to do all of her reading and writing under a massive electronic magnifier, I was moved by her generosity. It must have taken her over an hour to write me all those notes. When she asked me if I wanted to come back for tea, I told her to give me a call anytime.

Sitting in my car later, I scanned through the pages and teared up at the kind message she had left me. Participating in my research, she had written, gave her a sense of purpose and made her feel like her life had meaning.

Lorraine and I became friends, and I visited her once a week or so. I'd sit on her couch while she sat in her rocker, sipping water to try to quell her chronic dry mouth. We'd chat while CNN blared in the background. Lorraine loved all the worst CNN programs; *Nancy Grace* was her favourite. Lorraine loved to get all the juicy details on such stories as the disappearance of two-year-old Caylee Anthony in Florida. I spent hours grinning and bearing Nancy's piercing voice and big-ass hair. Besides the worst that CNN had to offer, Lorraine's other love was KFC. She would ask me to bring her some if I promised not to tell her nurse.

It was while standing over a bucket of the greasy stuff that my thesis really started to take shape. I had spent months poring over all my interviews. I'd spoken with eighteen women and had hours and hours of transcripts. The data was so rich and detailed, I could have easily written several PhD dissertations with the information I had. Overwhelmed by the sheer volume of the transcripts, not to mention the emotional toll of listening to hours of women sharing their struggles, I had become immobilized in my research. With too many options to choose from, I couldn't settle on a single thread to pull out and weave throughout my thesis.

But one day at Lorraine's, sitting on her couch gnawing on a chicken leg, I realized that the common theme throughout was the double bind of resilience. And suddenly, I was furious. I made up an excuse to cut my visit short and zoomed home to process my thoughts.

In my research, I had a record of the struggles of women fighting to make ends meet, crying over their inability to buy their grandkids Christmas presents. But they all took pride in being stoic. And as a result, their struggles were invisible. They were part of the "greatest generation" and were happily pulling themselves up by their bootstraps. Each woman insisted they knew someone who had it worse. They all insisted that their struggles weren't that bad.

Some, like Lorraine, were aware of the bind they lived in. Lorraine had told me that she wanted her situation to improve. She hated being lonely. She hated that she didn't get enough homecare service. But she also knew that no one likes a whiner. She knew that complaining would make her family come around less. She also knew that *not* complaining kept her struggles invisible. She couldn't win.

What I saw in my thesis was reflected in my work with sexual assault survivors. The few women who decided to report to police lived in a double bind. They had to look bad enough for their trauma to be taken seriously, but not be too much of a mess or else risk being seen as crazy and unstable. It wasn't enough that women were subjected to discrimination, violence, and neglect, I realized. We also had to perform our trauma in a very precise way in order to get any semblance of justice.

I was excited to finally have some direction in my research, but I had grossly underestimated the burden of carrying so many stories of struggle, not to mention the hours I spent on the support line. The weight of everyone's experiences was taking a toll on me. I'd regularly wake up at 4 a.m. in a cold sweat from a nightmare and then sleep through every alarm I set. A migraine sufferer since the eighth grade, I started getting migraines so severe that I experienced facial paralysis and projectile vomiting. I was nauseous all the time and popped Gravol like candy, while the people around me joked that I must be pregnant.

The cause of all my issues was obviously stress. I wasn't an idiot. I knew the pace of my life was unsustainable. But I refused to admit defeat. Everyone from my family to my thesis supervisor was on my ass to slow down and take better care of myself, but none of them had realistic solutions. My mom advised me to just admit I couldn't cut it in grad school and quit. James thought the solution was to hurry up and finish my damn thesis. Meanwhile, my thesis supervisor kept joking that I too would be an elderly woman by the time I was done studying them.

But I kept taking on more work, logging more hours, running myself into the ground. I created Canada's first chapter of the Hollaback! movement, a global network of activists organizing against street harassment. I organized protests to fight anti-choice policies and the lack of sexual assault evidence kits in hospitals. I was a machine.

Anytime I had a moment of quiet or the tiniest hint of a break, I would lie on the couch like a zombie, scrolling social media for hours. I'd sleep for twelve to fourteen hours at a time and wake up more exhausted than ever. I preferred the steady buzz of anxiety propelling me forward to the deep numbness I felt whenever I slowed down. So I'd get back to work. And there was no shortage of work for me.

The lobbying to get a sexual assault centre at Carleton was taking years rather than the few months we had anticipated. We had naively believed that asking the first woman president to create sexual assault services would be a slam dunk. But she was adamantly opposed from day one, so we had to keep switching up our tactics. A student referendum, petitions, protests, and letter writing took up hours and hours of my time.

Two years into our fight, we realized that we needed to start putting our politics into action and provide some semblance of support to survivors on campus, since the administration was nowhere to be found.

I called up my dad, who sent me a box crammed full of old cell phones that his work had planned to send to the recycling bin. I worked with a few other coalition members who had done peer support work to create a robust thirty-hour training guide. We trained all the other members on how to answer a support line. Then at four o'clock one morning, we put up dozens and dozens of posters on campus, advertising our new sexual assault support line.

The media paid attention and so did Xavier. Even though he no longer lived in Ottawa, he still kept tabs on me and the sight of my picture in the local paper gave him an excuse to reach out. Every victory felt like one step forward, two steps back.

I was running a support line while working two jobs and pursuing full-time studies. It was ridiculous. As the co-ordinator of the support line and the person whose name was on our bills, I was charged with transferring the line to the next person on call every four hours, 365 days a year. That meant being within cell phone reception at all times and stepping in should someone miss their shift. The support line didn't get that many calls, but we knew it was a lifeline for those who used it. We also knew that the administration would love nothing more than to shame us for not providing service as advertised. So we kept the phone line staffed from 8 a.m. to midnight, seven days a week.

By its nature, this work attracts people who are personally affected by sexual violence. Taking days of training to work countless unpaid hours on a support line isn't glamorous. It isn't CV building. It doesn't come with any street cred. The work is its own reward.

But to get the work done, you first have to survive your colleagues. As organizers and advocates, the Coalition for a

Carleton Sexual Assault Centre was incredible. We were effective at delivering our message, getting folks to join our cause, and using the media as our amplifier. This was before the Jian Ghomeshi trial and the #MeToo movement. Sexual violence wasn't yet dominating news cycles, but we successfully framed the conversation so that anyone who opposed what we were doing looked like a misogynist dinosaur.

Within the organization, though, things were a mess. I was good at managing the work and keeping the organization focused, but I was impatient and dismissive of my team members. I was worn thin from years of being overstretched and had no patience for those who wanted to take the group in a different direction. I was obsessed with reaching the finish line. All I wanted was a permanent safe space for survivors on campus. Anything else felt like a distraction, and I resented those who wanted to take us there.

Every time conversations came up about joining other student groups on campus or expanding our mandate, I lost it. I had such a sense of urgency about the work and constantly felt panicked that we were getting derailed. I resented everyone for not doing enough or caring enough.

We were a group of traumatized survivors working long hours with no pay and little validation for our efforts. We were toxic, mean, and petty. But we had no tools to cope with our own trauma, let alone the pain and suffering we took on from the survivors we were supporting. So we turned on each other.

The universe was throwing up countless red flags for me to slow down and get help, but I ignored them all. Every day, I bargained. *If I help one more person, maybe then I'll feel better.*

I never made the connection between the work I was doing and my life with Xavier. After all, it was examining myself through the lens of white privilege that had pushed me to start this work, not my own experience of abuse. And even though I was spending thousands of dollars on tuition to write a thesis on the complexities of resilience, it never occurred to me that my deep awareness of the issue came from my own lived experience. It was just what the data told me. I was just being a good listener.

It had been eight years since I'd left Xavier. It had been months since I'd heard from him. So, James and I made a deal. If 365 days went by without a word from him, we would consider it done. If a whole year went by without Dickwad popping into my life, then I could put it behind me and think of my stalker in the past tense. We made our deal over dinner at a local Thai place that I loved. We shook hands and made it official and then burst into laughter at the absurdity of it all.

Two weeks later, it was announced that I had won the Governor General's Award in Commemoration of the Persons Case. My dear friend Kate McInturff nominated me for all my work to end violence against women and to improve the lives of elderly women. It was an incredibly humbling experience to even be nominated, let alone chosen as one of five women that year. A prestigious award in recognition of women who've contributed to the fight for gender equality, it made the news. I did countless media interviews and my face was plastered on the front page of my hometown's newspaper.

Two weeks after I had celebrated the possibility of being rid of Xavier forever, my award brought him back into my life. He sent me a lengthy email to congratulate me.

There was nothing overtly menacing or sinister in the email. Most people would have read it as a kind message from an old friend. But it was the principle.

I knew it. He knew it.

I fell apart for a day or two, but I didn't want to seem ungrateful for the honour, so I shoved the email in a green folder where I stored all my notes from Xavier and carried on. I invited my family to the ceremony. They marvelled at the pomp and circumstance of Rideau Hall. My parents and grandmother took group photos with the Governor General and his wife. I got to give a speech under a massive painting of the Queen, wearing a suit I had custom ordered with my fancy new stilettos and a bright yellow tie. Part of the ceremony included being named in the House of Commons during question period, so I brought my Nana as my date and tried my best to let all the good soak in.

If I couldn't be rid of Dickwad, I wanted to do my best to forget him. I clung to the idea that denial was my only way out.

Police had told me he'd never stop. That damn counsellor on campus had told me he wouldn't stop either. My sense of terror waxed and waned, but it never went away. Because he never went away. Not really.

I had to tell myself that Xavier over my shoulder was a routine part of my life. I had to tell myself it wouldn't stop, because it was the only way to lessen the blow every time I heard from him.

Hey Julie,

I don't even know what to say in here, you've heard it all but won't go anywhere with it. I'm not here to harm you or make your life any tougher. I've had the hardest life since you left. I miss you to bits, I try and make things a little better between and seem to screw up everytime. It seems I'm done trying and I see that you're happy, or you look good and happy anyway, and even if you hate me the way I think you do, I'm still happy

to see that you're happy with your new chapter in your life. You always will, and still do have a special place in my heart. I miss you more than anything, but even if friendship won't an option, life goes on I suppose.

This card is in response to your "5 year old" card you gave me for my birthday, except you can choose how old you want to be in the card. Happy Birthday Julie!

I'm sorry for just "dropping in" like this again... I don't mean to freak you out. I'd knock if you were home, but that wouldn't make things any better, and I still have no real way of getting a hold of you.

I am continuously coming across a lot of your stuff, and figured some of these papers, you might wanted to keep... Like your cat's checkups and stuff at the animal hospital, for the dates and stuff, and what appears to be a few important information sheets coming from Carleton.

Either way, I'm not trying to freak you out, or not listen to your wishes, I'm simply giving you back your belongings.

6
Operation (Dis)honour

IN THE MID-EIGHTIES, MY FATHER HAD A SHORT BUT memorable military career as an infantryman. It was the fulfillment of a childhood dream. He'd grown up surrounded by family stories of his uncle's decorated infantry career, and his grandfather was a Toronto Highlander in World War II.

My father left the Canadian Armed Forces when I was a baby, so I'm too young to remember that life. But I spent my childhood being regaled with "mud puppy" stories. I've seen so many photos that my mind has filed them away as my own memories. There's one memorable photo of my baptism where my mom is rocking an incredible wide-brim teal hat with matching dress; she cradles my pure white lace-covered body as I wail. (I've never been a fan of church.) A priest is standing over me, about to pour water across my forehead because Catholics think innocent newborn babies need to be cleansed of eternal sins. In the background is my dad, donned in his military dress uniform, smiling broadly as he holds my older brother. My parents were twenty-one years old and so full of life. Their beauty and joy were unmistakable.

My father left the Forces after a few years because that life wasn't conducive to having a family. But he remained a dues-paying member of the Royal Canadian Legion and, for a while, was even in their marching band. Every November 11, my brother and I would stand on the sidewalk in the cold and watch my dad drum down the street in the Remembrance Day memorial march. We thought he looked like the Energizer Bunny in a kilt.

For grades eight and nine, my family moved to Manitoulin Island, where my brother, mother, and I spent two years as the only French people on the whole island. My accent was mocked by students and teachers alike, and I hated every second of it. But then I started high school, and my lanky, awkward teen self fell for Justin, a spirited ginger who shared my ambitious dream of getting the hell off the isolated island we called home. I wanted to be a journalist, and Justin wanted to join the Canadian Armed Forces.

We would go on to spend five years drifting in and out of each other's lives, cursed with bad timing. The rare times I was single, he was posted overseas. He would send me handwritten letters detailing how military life was everything he had hoped it would be, but he found the nights long and lonely. The man is gorgeous, so my crush never really went away. But we eventually conceded that a relationship was not in the cards for us and settled into being friends who would connect periodically and debate politics fiercely.

In the early 2000s, he had a short stint posted at Canadian Forces Base Petawawa, a two-hour drive from Ottawa. It was the closest we'd been in years, so I made plans to come up and visit. He was living in military housing, sharing the space with three other roommates. On a beautiful summer day, we all sat on the deck and chatted while I sipped ginger ale and they drank beer and shared a joint.

I had been around military men enough to know that trench humour is aptly named. I've had a potty mouth for as long as I can remember (sorry, mom) so their colourful language didn't shock me, no matter how hard they tried.

"I wish I could have bottled up the smell. There's honestly no way I could accurately describe to you the smell of that place. I remember it so vividly," Justin told me.

"Well, the smell of the country is one thing, but the smell of the morgue was fucking next level."

Listening to their casual discussions of morgue guarding duty and the horror of losing friends to war, I tried to play it cool. But I did find their casual brutality terrifying. And to think, these were the healthy ones. The lucky ones. They had come home after several tours of Afghanistan. Their limbs were intact and they were all on active duty. To these beautiful men, in the prime of their lives, babysitting the dead bodies of their colleagues while high on Afghani drugs was a funny anecdote. Survival is a funny thing.

. . .

ON A COLD, RAINY OCTOBER DAY IN 2014, I TOO WOULD be thrust into the chaos of military life. Because of my dad's and Justin's stories, I knew the military was unlike any other job out there. I wasn't naive about what the military environment did to people, especially men. But I was still filled with incredible optimism when the Royal Military College (RMC) in Kingston, Ontario, called me that spring to invite me to speak to all the cadets about sexual violence prevention.

After my work to get a sexual assault centre established at Carleton University, I had slowly started making a name for myself as an advocate and educator. After losing my job at a feminist non-profit as a result of funding cuts from the Conservative government, I got a contract to develop and manage a province-wide sexual violence campaign. With the help of a social marketing firm, I created an accessible bystander intervention campaign that focused on engaging bystanders to end sexual violence.

The job brought me all across Ontario, from elementary school classrooms to workplaces. I gradually shed my shyness, got more comfortable behind the microphone, and discovered a knack for getting folks engaged in discussion. Through a combination of humour and bluntness, I was able to get audiences to think critically about their role in ending sexual violence. I was having a blast.

After word got around about our great campaign, an English professor invited me to come to RMC to train teachers. That was in 2013. Colleges and universities were still reticent to acknowledge the high rates of sexual violence on campus, so I was excited to meet a handful of professors and administrators who were keen to get a conversation going on their campus. The presentation went really well and I drove home, thinking that was it.

The following May, I got a call from a captain at RMC who had heard great things about my presentation and wondered if I would be willing to come back to train all the cadets. I was floored. Never in my career had an entire institution committed to bystander training. It was unprecedented. She told me she would get back to me with dates, but that she was aiming for late September or early October.

I called my dad right away to share the good news. He shared my enthusiasm and thought it was a sign that the military was heading in a positive direction. I think his exact response was "Fuck yes!" I thought it was a real coup and said so on Twitter. I was pumped to spend the day talking to a thousand cadets, and although Twitter was quick to give me a sarcastic "Wow, good luck with that!" I felt prepared.

My dad had cautioned me that RMC was known for attracting some serious tight-asses. It was a prestigious institution where students, or cadets, as they are known, graduate with both a degree and rank. There was a clear distinction between those who came up through the ranks and the fancy pants who just went to RMC. Many of the cadets there came from prominent military families, and there was an obvious class divide between RMC students and the rest of the military. When I spoke to Justin about my upcoming gig, he referred to RMC students as "prissy pussies" who thought they were better than everyone else.

Based on the blunt feedback I was getting, I expected pushback from the cadets. When it comes to conversations on sexual violence, groups of mostly men are generally skeptical anyway. Add in the elitism of the institution and I fully expected them to be a challenge.

I had presented to highbrow places like private schools and government departments before. In my experience, they have enough tact to keep their resistance on the down low. Instead of engaging in outbursts or outright hostility, they are generally very quiet and show their disdain by sitting silently and refusing to engage in the discussion. It's a lot of cricket noises and awkward pauses.

So that's the expectation I brought to RMC on October 4, 2014, when I came to give presentations to all the cadets. The captain had worked hard to negotiate one session for each year, four in total, but the only date the school gave her was a Saturday. I wasn't jazzed to be working on a weekend, least of all on October 4, which is Sisters in Spirit day, a day of recognition for the high rates of missing and murdered Indigenous women and girls across Canada. Instead of attending a Sisters in Spirit rally, I was to be in Kingston for 7:30 a.m.

The moment I arrived, the captain came to greet me. We had never met in person, and so I greeted her with the usual "Nice to finally meet you." She responded in kind, but her smile quickly faded as she warned me that the cadets were upset with me.

I burst out laughing. "But I just got here! I haven't even said anything."

It seems that the school had failed to give the cadets much notice that they would have a mandatory training session on a Saturday. To make matters worse, it was the second or third working weekend in a row. A number of the cadets had purchased tickets to visit family for a couple of days and were now led to believe that the feminist educator lady was the reason they were stuck on campus, attending a presentation at eight in the morning.

Never mind that I didn't want to be there on a Saturday either. Never mind that it was never my idea. Never mind that they had booked me months in advance. No one corrected the rumour, and so they had it in for me before I even took the podium.

The captain walked me through the winding campus. I admired the incredible architecture. RMC is a beautiful campus, and though it was a cold and gloomy day, its impeccably manicured lawns and imposing buildings caught my eye. We walked to an old building, went up some stairs, and entered a grand hall with high ceilings and two hundred or so chairs arranged facing a podium and projector screen. It felt like a church.

The room was slowly filling up. As I approached the podium, I noticed an older man in uniform. His body language indicated he was important. He told me his name, which I promptly forgot (a terrible habit of mine). He thanked me for coming and said it was an important issue that they were glad to be featuring on campus. The captain took my USB key and began setting up my presentation, while I fidgeted with the microphone on the podium. That's when the important man informed me that the microphone wasn't working. I was waiting for him to follow up with what they were doing to address the situation, since I was to speak for the next eight hours to groups of two hundred people at a time. But instead I was instructed to "just yell at them. They're used to it." This was getting off to a great start.

I wore a blue dress with a row of buttons down the front that I loved and that made me look like I was a flight attendant from the sixties, which I didn't hate. I packed a pair of heels but arrived in my Hunter boots because it was pouring outside. Heels are a key part of my speaking uniform. I'm five foot ten but don't feel "on" as a presenter unless I'm wearing heels. Lipstick and heels are my armour when I'm in educator mode. But when the captain saw me pull out my heels, she gave me a look that said, *I wouldn't do that if I were you.*

At exactly eight o'clock, the captain called the group to attention and informed them that it was time to start. I waited on the sidelines as she introduced me, which is always the most awkward part of my job. Watching someone read out your accolades in the third person while you're standing right beside them never gets less weird. I had made sure to include my most prestigious bio, because I knew that establishing myself as an expert is a feat on a good day, but it's especially difficult with insular organizations like the military. I had never served. I was a civilian. I was a woman. And I was standing there in a blue dress, on a Saturday morning, talking to them about a taboo subject. I jammed that bio with every award I had ever won and ended with my recent Governor General's award. The Governor General is the figurehead of the Canadian Armed Forces, so I knew the award had weight in that space.

After the brief introduction, I got up. I don't speak with notes and the microphone was busted, so I abandoned the podium and just walked to the front of the room. Silently thanking my dad for teaching me how to yell from my gut, I projected the loudest voice I had. The sessions were to be ninety minutes long, but I was less than sixty seconds in when I knew I was fucked.

I start all my presentations with a little quip or joke to ease the inevitable tension in a room about to talk about rape. It's also my way of showing people that yes, I'm a feminist lady here to talk about this uncomfortable thing, but I'm *chill*.

I made a jokey comment about how delighted they must be to be talking about sexual assault at 8 a.m. on a Saturday. Even though I was clearly sarcastic, the joke fell flat. People stared directly at me with arms crossed. Here we go...

I went through every slide, outlining statistics on sexual violence and common myths. I threw out questions, each of which was met with deep, eerie silence. They were forced to physically be there, but no one had made them promise to participate.

I then launched into a discussion of bystander intervention and the reasons why people don't intervene. "The bystander effect," I joked, "is what's literally happening right now. You all know why people don't intervene, and none of you are saying anything because you're just hoping someone else answers the lady and gets you off the hook." That got a few chuckles. I thought maybe they were warming to me.

When we walked through two separate scenarios and I asked them how they would intervene, they were still quiet and seemed to answer with hesitancy, but at least there were some hands up. We ended fifteen minutes early because they were so damn quiet. The second I told them they were free to go, they bolted. One or two cadets from the far back of the room hung around. One spoke with the captain and the other came up to me.

This always happens. Speaking in front of a large group is nerve-racking for most of us, so it's common for people to approach speakers privately after speeches and presentations.

The cadet gave me the firm handshake I've come to expect from military members and thanked me for the presentation. He seemed shy and kept looking over his shoulder to make sure no one could overhear. He'd been sitting at the back of the room and couldn't hear very well, which he thought would perhaps explain why people weren't participating very much. "But, I won't lie," he said. "I also overheard people mumbling about how this whole thing was bullshit."

He went on to share that he had once been hanging out with a group of his guy friends in one of their rooms when they started talking about a female classmate. They all seemed to think she was hot. "But I didn't join in. I have a girlfriend," he quickly interjected.

The conversation soon turned to whether they would fight for her or take her all at the same time. Consent was clearly never part of the conversation, and as things got darker, he said something like "Okay, guys—enough," and they just laughed. "I realized I should probably report it to someone," he told me, "because what if they were serious, you know?" He kept looking around him as he spoke, which was my clue that the situation wasn't resolved in the best way possible. And sure enough, he told me that he had reported the incident weeks ago and nothing had been done about it.

I thanked him for trying and encouraged him to have a conversation, even a casual one, with the woman in question. "If it was me, I'd want to know that people were talking shit about me like that." He agreed, thanked me, and walked away.

Seeing the cadet walk away, the captain approached me to check in. "I'm sorry they were so quiet," she said. "I've never seen them like this before. Maybe it's because they're all new and have only been here a few weeks, so the topic freaked them out? I don't know. I could tell they weren't happy to be here, though. I'm sorry about that. You did great!"

I took a swig of my water bottle and braced myself for round two. The second group filtered in loudly. They were rowdy and jostled each other to try and occupy all the seats at the back of the room. Again, the captain called them to attention and introduced me, and away I went.

The strategy of the first group was to make me uncomfortable through eerie silence. This group took the opposite approach. They were loud and rambunctious, and because of the high ceilings and my lack of microphone, their whispers to each other meant I constantly had to stop and ask people to shut up so I could be heard. Most of the questions were answered earnestly, but they were also peppered with people saying outrageous things just to get a reaction from their classmates around them.

I looked out at the sea of uniforms. Although RMC includes army, navy, and air force, it was predominantly army camouflage and white, male faces looking back at me. The gender difference was stark, as was the lack of racial diversity. I was staring down a lot of agitated white dudes.

As I wrapped up the session, a sea of faces approached me, many of them women. I was excited to hear from them because I was dying to know how their experience at RMC was going. One woman insisted that the guys were immature but that they had never done anything serious to her. Another had filed a report in first year because of an "incident." But she quickly assured me it had been dealt with and she was "over it." But what all three of the women *really* wanted to tell me was that my content was great, my delivery was fine, but that I wasn't taken seriously by the cadets because I was a woman. "I just think that if they had a guy deliver the content, even another civilian, they would have paid more attention. They just don't listen to women around here."

I wasn't surprised to hear that, but hearing it from a woman shook me. I wanted to maintain the trust between us and appreciated that they were just trying to reassure me that I wasn't the problem, but I was angry. "You know that as women in this institution, that means they aren't going to listen to you either?" I replied. They sighed and couldn't disagree.

As the room cleared out, the captain and I noticed that a few of the cadets had left stuff behind. A beret, a few pieces of garbage. She was mortified. "They're not supposed to be walking across campus without their uniform in order and definitely not without a goddamn hat on their head. My God. What a shitshow this has been!"

It was now time to break for lunch. Although we hadn't discussed it beforehand, it's common practice to have a meal plan in place for speakers who have been engaged to work for eight hours. Not that day. The captain informed me that she needed to leave because of a lack of child care but that for the third and fourth sessions, a civilian colleague of hers from the counselling department would introduce me. She said goodbye, walked me to my car, and left me to my own devices.

I didn't know my way around Kingston and was so amped up from stress that I didn't have much of an appetite anyway. So I sat in my car, munched on some peanuts I had brought, and called my dad to vent.

He sounded truly disappointed and almost embarrassed. As a former military member, I suppose he felt they were a reflection of him and he didn't like the look. My dad's one of the best listeners I know, and I was grateful to be able to vent and blow off some steam before I walked in for another three hours of presenting.

I headed back to the hall that was already filling up. As I walked to the front of the room, I was catcalled. I don't remember the exact words, but they were about my body and involved a wolf whistle. I whipped my head back to look, and a group of men dramatically looked the other way and tried to stifle their laughter.

There was palpable energy in the room. I knew they were going to be an unruly group. The guy from counselling services came up to greet me and said nothing about the catcall. He either didn't hear it or didn't think it was noteworthy. He shook my hand, told me his name (which I promptly forgot), and asked if I was ready.

He called everyone to attention and only skimmed my bio, leaving out the awards and accolades. And then directed everyone to listen.

Right from the jump, they were a nightmare. I would get a sentence or two out and then have to stop and ask them to be quiet. They chattered incessantly.

The first section of my presentation was on the definition of consent, a word they thought was truly the funniest thing they'd ever heard. As I walked them through the Canadian Criminal Code definition of consent, they acted like I was a comedian just killing a set at the Comedy Cellar. It was so weird.

And disturbing. These were third-year students. A group made up largely of men in their early twenties and a straightforward, clinical, very unsexy lesson on consent made them so uncomfortable that they giggled like they were middle-schoolers sitting through sex ed. I wanted to take credit for all the epic zingers I was throwing down, but I wasn't trying to be funny. And they clearly weren't laughing *with* me, anyway. They wouldn't stop giggling and being noisy.

Around this time, a faculty member that I had met at my presentation the year before quietly entered the room. She was a civilian but was tough as nails. I knew right away when I met her that she took no shit. I kept presenting, and when we made eye contact, she smiled at me and gestured that she would just hang out at the back and watch.

The cadets either didn't notice her or didn't care. They didn't let up. Until I moved on to statistics.

I was there representing a provincial campaign on sexual violence against women. When RMC hired me, they knew that was my angle. They had seen me present the year before to faculty. I had a mandate to talk about the reality of sexual violence in Ontario, a province where one in three women will experience sexual violence in their lifetime.

The second I started reading out the statistics, their tone shifted from jokey to agitated. Consent was a gender-inclusive conversation, so although they had been determined to troll me, at least they were able to centre themselves. But even though I clearly framed the presentation as one about the role of bystanders, they were unbelievably offended that I was now talking about one in three women being sexually assaulted and not about men being assaulted and, in particular, about men being assaulted *by women.*

The slide literally read "One in three women will experience sexual violence in her lifetime." I didn't say "One in three women will be raped by a man" or "One in three women will experience sexual violence, which means one in three of you is a rapist." But they clearly didn't see it that way. Their hands shot up, so I called on one of the cadets sitting in the first few rows.

"Why are you only talking about women? Why aren't we talking about men? Are you saying you don't think men get assaulted? Are you saying you don't care?" As he spoke, his voice got louder and louder. Before I could answer him, the room erupted into cheers. They were yelling over each other. I tried in vain to shout over the crowd to calm down and let me answer the damn question.

I explained my mandate and informed them that he was basically outing himself as someone who didn't care about one in three women in Ontario. I was angry but kept my voice firm and steady. "And if you're actually concerned about men, know that one in six men will be sexually assaulted in their lifetime and the vast majority are sexually abused as children."

They seemed a bit taken aback but somewhat satisfied that I knew sexual violence against men existed. It was an odd moment. Nothing about their question denoted actual empathy for men who are assaulted, nor did they act in a way that showed me they would respond to the abuse of a man with any empathy. I mean, they laughed through a conversation about consent, but they wanted me to believe they were the true allies of victims in that room? I wasn't buying it.

Things got a bit better when we moved on to scenarios. I'm sure it helped that the first one was a bit of a softball. I asked them what they would do if a friend sent them someone else's nudes. Even though I had zero confidence that they actually believed what they were saying, they were of the generation where sexting was normalized, and so they knew the right answer was to delete the photos and not send them on to other people. A few people answered in earnest, and I thought I had finally gotten them on track and listening.

And then I brought in the issue of alcohol. The next scenario was about alcohol-facilitated sexual assault, based on the fact that over half of sexual assaults in Canada involve booze in some way. The slide read: "Your friend stumbles out of the bar with some guy. Do you stay and keep dancing?"

They immediately started laughing. I knew that homophobia and machismo had them balking at the idea that they would dance at a bar. I'd had a similar reaction in past presentations to groups of largely men. So I asked them to quiet down and replace dancing with grabbing another drink, playing another game of pool, whatever it is they did at the bar.

After each scenario, I gave them a few minutes to chat with the people around them before I brought the discussion to the big group. Their discussions were unbelievably loud. It took me a solid minute to get their attention back when it was time to share as a group.

I thought the laughing at the beginning was strictly about the dancing part of the scenario. But it turns out, many had chosen to read the situation as a drunk man being dragged out of the bar by another man. The same group that had accused me of being indifferent to the sexual violence men face were now openly mocking the idea that a man would be sexually assaulted.

Someone put their hand up and asked for clarification. They had read the scenario as intended, with the woman as the one being dragged out of the bar by some guy. "Was that correct?" a cadet asked me in a tone that felt genuine.

"Yes, that's the way we thought of it. But if you switched the roles, that's okay too, I guess. But yes, you're right. We meant that a *female* friend of yours stumbles out of the bar with some guy."

Then all hell broke loose. They all erupted into chatter again. It took every ounce of patience I had to remind them for the umpteenth time that I didn't have a microphone and they needed to only speak when I called on them.

A cadet sitting near the front with a cocky grin put his hand up. When I called on him, he began to explain to me in the most condescending voice imaginable that I, and my work, was very misguided. He dramatically waved his arms around the room. "As you can see from looking around the room, we're mostly guys here. So why are we talking about what happens to women? As a man, I'm offended. It seems to me that you just don't care about men."

The room erupted. Neither the professor who had snuck in to sit at the back nor the man who had introduced me intervened. How do you defend yourself in a moment like that? I did my best. I reminded him of the statistics. I reminded him of the women sitting right fucking beside him. I reminded him that these were transferable skills. None of it mattered. They shouted and jeered that I was a man hater. I had officially lost the room.

They were shouting over each other and interrupting me. I wasn't able to move on because they just wouldn't shut up. It was chaos.

After several exasperated pleas of "C'mon, people, be quiet for one goddamn second," they startled settling down. Their hands stayed up, though. One hand in particular belonged to one of the few sailors in the room. In his white uniform, he stuck out in the room of mostly camouflage. He was smack dab in the middle of a particularly rowdy group sitting near the front. No part of me wanted to invite cadets to keep speaking, but I also knew that if I didn't call on someone who'd had their hand up for a while, I would be inviting criticism of a different kind. Loud and obnoxious people love to act as though they're being censored. So in spite of myself, I called on the sailor to share.

To my astonishment, he unleashed in the best way. "Ma'am, pardon my language, but the way men talk about women here at RMC is fucking disgusting."

His words landed in the room with a bang. Suddenly, the room went silent. I was ready to high-five him with my whole heart for just that one sentence, but he wasn't done. After a long pause, he went on. "The fact that I have to sit here and listen to you guys go on and on about how you're *so* offended that she's talking about women and not men is fucking embarrassing. She's not talking about men getting raped because it's not men being raped, and everyone in this room fucking knows it. Can you all please just shut the hell up and let her do her goddamn job?"

His rage was delicious. Stepping into the obvious awkwardness his words had created, I thanked him for his input and attempted to move on. As I pivoted back to the podium to switch the slide, I noticed another hand shoot up on the other side of the room. *Oh, damn!* I thought. *The allies have finally come out to play.*

I called on him only to be met with "Ma'am, if I'm drunk and she's drunk, then who's the rapist?"

Fuck my life. My moment of zen was short-lived as the crowd got rowdy again. I was back to square one.

I tried to inform my latest troll, and his rowdy comrades, that from a legal perspective, neither person is able to give or receive consent, which means you are both on the hook for possible charges. But from a moral perspective, the issue I cared about was harm. And if you're entering into a sexual situation questioning "Am I committing a crime?" then your sex life is problematic to say the least.

I could tell that the root of the question was "How do I avoid getting into trouble?" So I said that the simplest answer was, "If you're not sure if someone's too drunk to consent, then assume they are too drunk to consent. If all you're concerned about is covering your own ass, then do not pass go."

I thought that answered the question, but on they went, questioning when they needed to have empathy for women who drank too much. One guy even went so far as to try to say that if he got drunk at a bar and was stabbed to death on the way home, "*obviously* everyone would know it was my fault for being drunk and alone on the street."

I literally laughed and asked him to give me a single example of that victim blaming ever happening. He had nothing, but that didn't stop his classmates from yelling over each other that he was right.

Although my instinct was to kick over the podium and scream at them, I was at work. I had been asked to facilitate four trainings, and I was going to facilitate four trainings. Bailing on work has never been my style. It never occurred to me to walk out. I was determined to rise above their bullshit and fulfill my commitment. But it was the longest ninety minutes of my life.

When the session finally ended, there was some half-hearted clapping, while most of the room stormed out. One cadet from the rowdy group sitting near the front walked up to me, looked me up and down, and whispered, "I *might* have listened to you if you weren't a woman and a civilian," turned on his heels, and walked out. I had hoped that my ally the sailor would come up to me and say something, but he stormed out of the room too.

A small group of women did stick around to chat. They all seemed pretty mortified by what had happened. "Please know that lots of people agreed with you, but like, we were clearly outnumbered so it was hard to say anything."

I asked them if they knew the sailor who had tried to stick up for me. They didn't know his name but they'd seen him around campus. "Do you agree with his comments about the way men talk about women around there?" I asked.

It turns out, they hadn't given it much thought until the week or so before the training. It seems they'd been notified via email about the training session, and the email included my name. Some of the male cadets had googled me and "made a bunch of rapey jokes about you and how you probably hated men."

The cadets had literally made rape jokes about the anti-rape educator who was coming to teach them not to rape. Cool, cool.

Lots of folks seemed concerned about the violent attitude of the cadets, but only one person had stood up to say so. What had that sailor heard, or witnessed, that compelled him to break from the pack in such a big way? Why hadn't the counsellor intervened?

After the room cleared out, he came up to me, looking visibly uncomfortable. "Well, they sure seemed to have a lot of questions!" he said with a laugh.

"I can't imagine being a woman at this school. Jesus Christ," I replied, stone-faced.

"Yeah, it got a bit heated there a few times. But I think it was a good discussion and you seemed to handle it all in stride. Otherwise, I would have interjected."

Seems it was just a regular day at RMC for this guy. Thankfully, I only had one session left. *Ninety more minutes. Just ninety more minutes,* I repeated to myself as I pretended to dig through my purse for something. As I tried to look busy, an older man in full camouflage approached me. He introduced himself as a leader to the fourth years and as "an ally to the cause." He informed me that he was going to stay to watch the session because he thought it was "such an important topic," but also because he knew that his presence in the room sent a message. "I do not doubt your capabilities," he said, "but I want to be present, if that's all right with you."

It was more than okay with me. Perhaps the presence of an older ranked military official was the ticket to getting the cadets to behave. He also informed me that fourth years have rotating cadets in supervisory roles and asked if it was all right for the current supervisor to open with a few words. At this point, I thought, *I'll try anything.* I told him it had been a trying day and so I appreciated his presence and introductory remarks.

Once the room had filled up and the two men gave their "This is important—pay attention" speeches, I was off to the races.

Looking out at this room of two to three hundred uniforms, with the pomp and circumstance of vaulted ceilings and gilded window frames, I realized I hadn't been fully present all day. I had subconsciously dissociated at some point and had simply been going through the motions. I had created the content and been facilitating it for years, so without knowing it, I was working from muscle memory. By this point, it was late afternoon. I had been "on" for almost eight hours. I was exhausted and my patience was wearing thin. Staring down the last ninety minutes of my contract, I decided, *carpe diem.*

Since the guy from counselling services had failed to introduce me, I had the perfect opportunity to frame the discussion. I squared my shoulders, planted my feet, and introduced myself as an award-winning public educator and expert on violence against women "who is, frankly, deeply disappointed in RMC." Cadets visibly sat up to attention. "I have been working to end violence against women in Canada since 2003. I've given literally hundreds of workshops and I've trained thousands of people. I teach this *exact* content to middle-schoolers and they are better behaved than you folks have been today. This is a prestigious institution. I was told it was an honour for me to be invited here. But I'm not impressed. If you want me to leave here respecting the importance of RMC, then impress me."

It was a bold move. It was the direct opposite of my usual jokey introduction. I wasn't trying to warm up the room. I was setting a boundary. And for a while, it worked.

They paid attention or at least faked it well. They participated whenever I asked a question. One cadet went so far as to ask how he could teach the tools I was giving them, "since we're all months away from being leaders ourselves."

I started to sense some rumblings from a few cadets sitting in front to my left. It was nowhere near the nonsense from earlier, so I didn't plan on drawing too much attention to it. But it didn't matter. The older ranked member spotted a cadet and quietly walked up to his row, gestured to him, and instructed him to stand at the front, facing the rest of the crowd. It was an old-school disciplinary tactic of humiliating the offending party, and boy, did it work. He stood to the side of the room, at full attention, rocking a deep shade of scarlet. He didn't say a word for the rest of the session. Grateful to be dealing with grown adults for the first time all day, I ended the session with a long thank-you for their earnest participation and clear commitment to the issue.

A few cadets approached me after the session to thank me for coming. They seemed to find the information helpful and particularly appreciated my impromptu discussion about the best ways to transfer these skills to others. I only had one weird interaction with a cadet who came up holding a small notebook. He had written out several questions and wanted me to go through each one, but they were all super weird, like, "What is your opinion of the Rehtaeh Parsons case?"

Rehtaeh Parsons was a young woman who had been sexually assaulted at a party a few years before, and after photos of the assault had circulated at school, she was harassed so badly that she took her own life. It had nothing to do with military life, and the case hadn't been brought up at all during the session. And besides, what hot take could I possibly have had?

He also asked me about rates of false reporting (they're very low) and whether I thought it should be a criminal act to make a false report (it is). He had that tone I have come to recognize as "sophisticated troll." They don't come right out and call your views offensive or man hating. They instead try to lay a bunch of traps for you to fall into. And they love a good "But what about…"

I sensed the older ranked man hovering in the corner, waiting for me to finish. I appreciated that I hadn't been left alone with this troll and did my best to answer his questions as succinctly as possible, while also letting him know that he seemed to be seeking out a debate or lengthy discussion and I just didn't have the time. "I put my email up on the screen. Feel free to email me if you'd like to continue this conversation. But it's been a long day and I have a two-hour drive home, so I'm going to have to go now."

The cadet seemed disappointed, but I didn't care. I wanted the fuck out of there.

The last session was the best of them all, but I hadn't forgotten how tense things had been up to that moment. I knew there was a silent group of people in each session who had agreed with me but felt unsafe to say so. I knew there were survivors in each session, of all genders, who'd felt supported by my message.

But I also knew there were cadets in the room who had joked about raping me before I'd even showed up. So when it was time for me to pack up and leave, I pretended to be lost.

It wasn't a complete lie. The campus was confusing and I wasn't entirely sure how to make my way back to the highway.

I asked the kind older man who had come to supervise if he could show me back to my car. He happily obliged and directed me to the closest gas station and highway exit. I took my first real deep breath on the drive home and called my dad to vent.

It's a short drive from Kingston to Ottawa, and I came home to a full house. It was a UFC fight night. Since I had both a deep love of combat sports and a projector television, I routinely hosted. I gave my friends a quick rundown of how the day had gone, changed into comfier clothes, and settled onto the couch to watch the fights.

I had talked on Twitter about my upcoming visit to RMC so I thought it made sense to post an update. My contract with RMC was finished the second I walked off campus, so I figured, *I'll never have to see these people again. Might as well be honest.* And I was.

I knew other potential employers were listening, so I held back a bit. But I didn't shy away from naming how awful the day had been and how, as a public educator on sexual violence, I can't help but assume the worst about men who are defensive and angry when being told that violence against women is real. It was a version of something I said on a weekly—if not daily—basis on Twitter.

My entire Twitter account was about violence against women and my blunt takes on the issue, so no one following me was taken aback or surprised. In fact, most of them had an "I told you so" attitude to my experience that day. Many had tried to quash my enthusiasm when I first announced I got the contract. Eventually, I put my phone down, hung out with my friends, and quickly filed the whole thing away as A Really Bad Day at Work.

On the advice of my friends, I woke up the next day and sent a kind, but blunt, email to the captain who had invited me. There was no formal complaint process available to me, but I thought I should at least let her know how things went after she left. It was a Sunday morning, so I didn't expect to hear anything for a while. Still, I figured it was worth noting that the cadets were not only extremely disrespectful to me, but they also said some truly disturbing things that had me concerned about the culture on campus. I ended my email by saying it had been a really difficult day but that I was committed to returning to RMC, should I be invited, because I believe in this work and it's clear that much work needed to be done.

On Monday, I awoke to a phone call from the captain. I naively assumed she had read my email and was calling to apologize. Instead, she immediately popped off on me, telling me that she had been pulled into her superior's office that morning and informed that multiple cadets had filed complaints against me, accusing me of calling all cadets rapists. She said I'd slandered the institution online, and as a result of my behaviour, *she* was facing reprisal because she had invited me.

I was stunned. My suspicion was that the worst offending cadets in my presentations sensed that I was going to file a complaint against them, so they tried to beat me to the chase. Since they had access to the chain of command and I didn't, they fired off complaints right away on Saturday, two days before anyone would have heard my side of the story. Not content to rest there, they googled me and screen-grabbed my tweets, turning them into some narrative about how I had publicly declared that "all cadets at RMC are rapists."

Never mind that I never deleted a single tweet, so a simple search would have disproven their accusations. The story was, "She came here to goad us into being angry with her. Then she blasted us online and damaged our reputations." That was the story they told, and that was the story that stuck.

No part of me wanted the captain to get into trouble or lose her job, but I had absolutely nothing to apologize for. I reminded her that my contract ended the second I left campus, that my contract made it very clear that I was not an employee of RMC, and that freedom of expression is real. I was a civilian who was not told to keep the day's events confidential, so I had done absolutely nothing wrong. And in fact, I was the one who was owed an apology.

I could hear panic in her voice. To me, it felt like she knew the day had gone badly, but all her concerns about that went out the window when her job was on the line. I can't say I blamed her. So we were at an impasse. She told me she would share our conversation with her superiors and get back to me.

When I logged on to Twitter, it was a garbage fire. Cadets, with their full names and real photos, going off about how I hate men and that my presence on campus was part of a plot to take down the military. They told me they were "very disappointed," as though they were my mom scolding me for skipping curfew.

Not enough for cadets to spam my account on their own, the girlfriends of RMC cadets got in on the fun too. One in particular spent hours going around in circles with me, acting as though she was just a member of the community concerned that I had painted such a prestigious institution in a bad light. A quick scan of her Twitter feed showed that she was in fact dating an RMC cadet. When called on it, her account went quiet. The tweets and accusations went on for hours.

The next day, the captain called me to say that she had shared my email with her superiors and they would be investigating. I told her that if RMC was so worried about their reputation, they should probably rein in the cadets who were making asses of themselves and libelling me in the process. Less than an hour later, all the accounts went dark.

Although the Royal Military College had paid for my travel and hotel, they hadn't paid me a fee. Because I was there in my role as co-ordinator of a provincially funded campaign, schools incurred no cost but my travel. Which means that I didn't even get paid extra for this nonsense.

Being provincially funded, I thought I should do my due diligence and notify my funder of what happened, lest RMC contact them or the story go public. This was the fall of 2014. #MeToo had not yet happened. Everyone doing this kind of work knew that the world was hostile and resistant.

Thankfully my funder was incredibly supportive. But they were also torn. It was clear from what had happened that RMC needed my voice and the content we provided. But it also meant feeding me to the wolves. While RMC "investigated" (a process I was not looped in to, so I had truly no idea what it entailed), the threats kept rolling in. The story hadn't hit the news, so it was clear that whoever was sending me nasty tweets and messages was connected to the campus in some way.

Opening up my Twitter app would send my heart racing. I got a lot of support from my followers, but it didn't ease the panic I felt every time a new message came in. To make matters worse, a mere two weeks after my infamous day at RMC, the Jian Ghomeshi story broke. A once beloved CBC radio host and musician, Ghomeshi was accused by a number of women of being a sadistic abuser who got off on humiliating women in the workplace and punching his dates in the face. It was absolutely scandalous, and it set off a firestorm of controversy and conversation.

Suddenly, the issue that my colleagues and I had spent decades quietly toiling away at was the main story in every media outlet and on every social media platform. My sector was inundated with media requests. Our social media accounts were flooded by allies and trolls alike. And our workload doubled, if not tripled.

Women were coming out of the woodwork to call out the abusers in their own lives. It felt like we were pulling back the giant boulder that had been sitting on our chests for centuries and watching all the bugs scurry away, seeking shelter. It was Canada's precursor to the global #MeToo movement, which took off in 2017 when Hollywood producer Harvey Weinstein was outed as an abuser. In Canada, the Ghomeshi trial sparked a movement of women sharing stories of sexual violence in the arts world, on campus, in politics, in their faith communities, and in their relationships.

Around the same time, a video went viral around the globe of actor Shoshana Roberts wearing a hidden camera, walking around New York City and being street-harassed at an astounding rate. The video, known as "Ten hours of walking in NYC as a woman," showed Roberts being catcalled 108 times in ten hours. It sparked an explosion of conversation around sexual violence that was both incredible and overwhelming.

As an established advocate for sexual violence survivors, I was targeted by every troll imaginable who didn't give a shit about Jian Ghomeshi prior to this moment but suddenly felt like an attack on him was an attack on all men. "Innocent until proven guilty!" they spouted, repeatedly, from as many troll accounts as they could manage. I was drowning.

My funder and my board of directors could see, in real time, how I was flooded with both legitimate media interviews and requests for presentations, and attacks from haters. And since I worked alone, at home, several hours away from the rest of the team, I was isolated. I didn't even have a supervisor. The day I was at RMC, or at any of my other talks, no one knew where I was or what I was doing. Until that point, the freedom felt like I was living the dream. But my experience at RMC also showed me how dangerous things were. I was completely alone.

They decided to pull together some funding so that I could get clinical supervision, which is a fancy way of saying "We're hiring you a therapist." The funding came in not a moment too soon, as I received a letter from the commandant of RMC, thanking me for coming to his campus. The page-long letter detailed how valuable the presentations were and how my expertise was greatly appreciated.

It did not mention my complaint. It did not include an apology. It was like he was referring to a completely different person or series of events. It was unreal.

My employer responded by demanding a meeting with RMC to go over what had happened to me and to develop a plan for moving forward, since it was evident that issues ran deep on the campus. In response, the commandant wanted a simple phone call. We wanted everything in writing and insisted on an in-person meeting. They negotiated back and forth, all while we were being told of an "investigation" in broad terms. I felt like complete shit.

My one bad day at work was turning into an avalanche of bad days. Between the online mob, the constant media requests, and the demand for more and more presentations, my body checked out. I had flu-like symptoms for months. I slept poorly. I had constant nightmares. I felt completely numb. Even if I spent a full day with friends, leaving my phone on mute and never checking my inbox, I was unable to feel deep joy.

Getting funding from my employer to see a therapist was the first step, but finding one was another story. Because I had spent years doing front-line peer support work, I had interacted with a lot of mental health workers in the city. It was difficult to find someone that I did not already know. The next hurdle was finding a therapist who knew how to support someone who had supported others. Providing therapy to someone who has experience in the field is a specialized skill set. And then, once I'd narrowed that down, I had to find a therapist who was even accepting new patients. I called around and doctor after doctor told me they either weren't accepting new patients at all or not for another six to eight months.

Exasperated, I told myself I'd try one more doctor and if that didn't work, I'd give up. And that's how I found Dr. Lynn. She had experience working with folks in the healing fields, a short waiting list, and an office at a convenient location. I was delighted.

At twenty-nine years old, despite everything I had been through, it was my first experience going to therapy. We would meet up every two weeks or so, and I would vent about the stresses of work and how I was struggling.

What I was going through on the work front was objectively terrible, so my response to it (numbing, anxiety, nightmares) was perfectly normal. But Dr. Lynn suspected the last few months were also triggering an old wound. I never mentioned Xavier. Not because I was being coy or secretive. I legitimately didn't make the connection. Denial had carried me through for so long that it never occurred to me that the constant surveillance of online trolls combined with the stress of talking about violent men for hours at a time, day after day, would trigger me.

I made a flippant comment at one point about "an old boyfriend who's been stalking me for years," and I think I even threw in an eye roll for effect. Her face showed surprise but she didn't press. It never even occurred to me to open up that old wound at that point. I was just trying to survive the immediate fire in front of me.

Months had gone by since my day at RMC, and the commandant and my employer continued their ping-pong letter exchange. It seems RMC had been investigating *me* and not the cadets, and via letter, they grilled me for information to back up my claims of sexist comments and disclosures from survivors. We refused to out survivors, they told us we were being unco-operative, and things continued back and forth.

Finally, five months after that infamous day, RMC wrote us one last letter, acknowledging that I had been harassed that day at RMC. In one of our letters to them, I had outlined how concerned I was that a captain was facing reprisal or possible dismissal for inviting me. They admitted that it was on the table but said that I should rest assured that her job was safe. Finally, they said that an investigation had backed up my claims that second and third years had been the worst, and that they had been punished. I should have been elated, but in the chaos of my post-Ghomeshi workload, it barely registered as good news.

Especially since post-Ghomeshi Canada was naming and shaming every sector of society that had issues of sexual violence, and the Forces were next. Around the same time that I received my final correspondence from RMC, former Supreme Court justice Marie Deschamps released a scathing report on the rates of sexual violence in the Canadian Armed Forces. Her section on RMC quoted one cadet as saying that if she reported every time she experienced sexual harassment, it's all she would do all day.

Deschamps's report was a bombshell, and the Chief of the Defence Staff, General Tom Lawson, didn't shy away from dismissing her and her findings. The Forces challenged her methodology and said they would need to take some time to decide if they accepted her recommendations.

Having witnessed the power of whistleblowers over the past few months, I knew that the lack of survivors coming forward to back up Justice Deschamps was deliberate. When the Ghomeshi story broke, women came out of the woodwork to back up the three victims who formally reported him. When two federal NDP staffers anonymously came forward about being sexual harassed by two Liberal MPs, women of all stripes came forward to share their stories of harassment on the Hill.

I knew that women were out there, wanting to talk about the conditions in the military. But I also knew that it wasn't safe for them. A military life is exactly that—your whole life. The military decides where you sleep and what underwear you're allowed to wear. The idea that you could easily denounce something and go back to work the next day unharmed is ridiculous.

But I was a civilian. I had written proof that I had been harassed. I had a job that supported me. I had a Governor General's award recognizing my expertise.

So I used my connections and poked around, eventually finding the name of a journalist who came highly recommended as an ally. James Cudmore worked for the CBC, was ex-military, and had been known to cover tough stories on military culture. He was very interested in my story and wanted to meet.

I liked him right away and felt I could trust him, especially because he didn't mince words. "If we do this, is there anywhere you could go? Maybe leave the country for a bit?" he asked me, as we strolled along the pedestrian bridge downtown on a hot spring day.

As always, I called my dad for advice. He didn't mince words either. "As your father, I don't think you should do it. People are going to come down on you hard and I don't think it's safe. But as a human being, and someone who has learned so much from your work, you have to do it. You teach people bystander intervention and the importance of taking the harder path. You can't back down now."

I set up an interview with James the next day. It was a short walk-and-talk interview on a bright, sunny day. It didn't feel any more stressful, or even more important, than any of the other hundreds of interviews I'd done in my career. It was taped for CBC's nightly news program *The National*. It wouldn't air for a bit, so he promised to keep me posted. I went back to work and tried to keep my head above water, all the while drowning in work.

The short clip aired across the country on a Thursday evening in May. Then it went to CBC's online desk and clips began playing on the radio. Media requests started pouring in, and the next day, I did back-to-back interviews with various outlets, in English and French, for over twelve hours.

Years of repression have given me an incredible ability to run on autopilot. I talked in detail, over and over again, about the events of October 4 and the subsequent fallout, and felt nothing. Before my last interview, I ran into James Cudmore in the hallway. He pulled me aside, looked me in the eye, and asked, "How are you doing? You know you can say no at any time. You don't owe anyone anything." I was touched by his kindness but felt an irrepressible urge to capitalize on this tiny sliver in time when people actually cared.

The media interviews were a lot, but they paled in comparison to social media. I received thousands of tweets and retweets. I got over a hundred emails in one day. As I scrolled through my inbox, I got email after email telling me I was a lying bitch, with some kind emails from allies peppered in. I also got dozens and dozens of emails from current and former Canadian Armed Forces members, of all genders, saying, "It happened to me too."

Doing interviews in multiple languages gets you threats in multiple languages. What fun! One such email was titled "Vous êtes une poubelle comme être humain." It detailed how I was an attention whore and that unfortunately people were paying attention but, thankfully, only for fifteen minutes. I was disgusting and an embarrassment to women everywhere. The writer also made clear that attacking me in this way was not misogynist because I'm not a person—I'm trash. Such garbage that I should do the world a favour and kill myself. He signed the email with his full name and mailing address.

CBC did a follow-up story where I read aloud threats I had received in the hope that it would wake people up to the reality that women have a lot of incentive to stay quiet. None of the threats were deemed serious enough for criminal charges. I had to just sit there and take them.

My whereabouts were discussed openly on 4chan and Reddit. Someone uploaded a lengthy YouTube video outlining how I was part of a feminist conspiracy to take down the military. A man called my cell phone and threatened me. He had a fixation on me that included lengthy blog posts about how I was a misandrist cunt who made up being a victim for money and fame, but I was also hot, so he wanted to rape me more than kill me.

At one point, my photo ended up on a website called Punchable Faces, where men debated whether I should be punched in the face, with some disagreement as to whether I should be raped first. Turns out, they hated me but thought I had a pretty face. This moment gave birth to what I've since called "confused boner," where men really, really don't like me and what I stand for but also want to fuck me, and their poor brains can't figure out what to do next. I had to find ways to laugh, because the truth was unbearable.

Even my beloved Justin, longtime crush and confidant, turned on me. He accused me of painting all military men with the same brush and quoted online misogynist "red pill" type nonsense at me. "More whining from weak people who should not be in alpha societies. If you were being a cunt and they called you a cunt, that's not harassment. That's just them being honest." I was crushed.

It was too dangerous for me to speak in public unaccompanied, so I could only agree to a presentation if the organizer could provide me with a security detail. Whether in school auditoriums or hotel conference rooms, I spoke while flanked by men with weapons. It was days and days of constant attacks. At one point, a man got close enough to me at one of my talks to tell me he was watching me.

I wanted so badly to seem brave and unbothered. I didn't want to give any of the assholes the satisfaction of knowing they were getting to me. So I tweeted snarky responses. I wore my highest heels and brightest lipstick and gave talks as though it was no big deal. Trying in vain to calm my worried parents,

I assured them it sucked but it was bearable. I maintained a pleasant aura of deep denial.

It turns out that around the same time as the Deschamps report, General Lawson announced his retirement. He agreed to an exit interview with Peter Mansbridge, then the lead anchor on CBC's *National*. During the interview, Mansbridge asked him specifically about what had happened to me.

Even though his own staff had written me a formal apology, even though a five-month investigation backed up my claims, General Lawson said my presentation resulted in a great discussion and that what really happened was a matter of perception. The cadets found it challenging, but educational. He gaslit me on national fucking television.

But that part of the interview got buried in the mix, because when Mansbridge followed up with a question about the root causes of sexual misconduct, General Lawson actually said, "It's because we are biologically wired in a certain way."

I had just landed in Winnipeg when the interview aired. I was due to speak at a conference the next morning. But instead, I ducked in and out all day, granting countless interviews that responded to Lawson's claims. He was condemned in the House of Commons by every party. Even Conservative prime minister Stephen Harper put aside his usual "support the troops" stance to side with me in denouncing Lawson's comments. It was a shitshow.

It had been nearly nine months since I'd presented at RMC. The Ghomeshi story still dominated every headline. My workload saw no signs of stopping. To make matters worse, my parents told me they were separating.

I finally conceded to my therapist that I was struggling. Tired of putting up a front everywhere I went, I made a deal with myself that Dr. Lynn's office was one place where I could be real with myself. She very gently went back to my nonchalant reference to a stalker, and I gave her the highlights in a detached, unemotional tone. She suggested that this Xavier character might be what was making everything so difficult to handle, since it was an obvious trigger to my feelings of surveillance and constant scrutiny. I didn't want to go there but I forced myself to at least consider the possibility.

Spring turned to summer, and my thirtieth birthday arrived. I had always wanted to go skydiving, so I convinced a group of friends to come with me. Strapped to the front of a bubbly Frenchman named Maurice, I jumped out of a plane and felt the incredible adrenaline rush. When I landed, I would have had enough energy to push the car all the way home.

Arriving to a house full of people, I should have been elated. So many people had come out to celebrate my birthday, and my parents had insisted they were on good terms and should visit. I had a house full of people who cared about me. Instead of letting that sink in and wash away the negativity and hate of the last while, I crashed. My adrenaline immediately plummeted and gave way to intense numbing. I felt completely alone and ended up spending an hour in the bathroom upstairs, curled in a ball as my friends and family partied downstairs.

At 1 a.m., I got an email from Xavier, apologizing for missing my birthday by a whole hour. I walked into therapy the next week determined to find a way to deal with him. "I tell myself I'm fine. I tell myself it's not a big deal. And then I hear from him and I just want to *die*. It feels like I'm right back to where I started. So I tell myself it's never going to end and then everyone tells me to stop being so pessimistic. So I cycle back to getting my hopes up and then he contacts me again and I live that cycle over and over again."

Dr. Lynn listened patiently and then leaned in to validate that I was right—he'll probably never stop. "You can't control him," she reminded me. "Lord knows you've tried, but you can't. All you can control is how you react to him. So I'm here to sit with you and acknowledge that this has gone on too long and it will go on even longer and it's not okay and it's not your fault."

My body thawed just the slightest amount, and I cried and cried.

The backlash was endless. Xavier was resolute. I was thirty years old and needing to make peace with the truth that there was no end in sight. I would never escape that day at RMC. I'd never escape dating (and leaving) Xavier. This was my life now.

ROYAL MILITARY COLLEGE OF CANADA · COLLÈGE MILITAIRE ROYAL DU CANADA

PO Box 17000, Station Forces · CP 17000, Succursale Forces · Kingston, Ontario · K7K 7B4

1045-1 (DDCdts)

28 October 2014

Julie Lalonde

Dear Madam:

I would like to thank you for taking the time to provide your briefing and insights on **Sexual Violence and Bystander Intervention** to the Cadets of the Royal Military College of Canada. This is an important topic for me, and one that I recognize requires open and frank discussion. I would like to specifically thank you for spending your entire day at the College to ensure that the majority of our Cadets were afforded the opportunity to hear your views and perspectives.

I appreciate that it is an extremely challenging topic to present in a university environment where students can pose difficult questions, and they often have perspectives that benefit through shared discussion. As such, I wish to acknowledge your efforts in stimulating dialogue and discussing bystander intervention.

Once again, I would like to thank you for your efforts in bringing this important topic to the Cadets of the Royal Military College of Canada. I wish you much success as you continue to bring your message to audiences across the country.

Sincerely,

A.D. Meinzinger
Brigadier-General
Commandant

ROYAL MILITARY COLLEGE OF CANADA · COLLÈGE MILITAIRE ROYAL DU CANADA

PO Box 17000, Station Forces · CP 17000, Succursale Forces · Kingston, Ontario · K7K 7B4

4 February 2015

Dear ███████████,

I was very pleased to have the opportunity to speak with you by telephone. I regret the misunderstanding about the location of our meeting and, as indicated to you, I will continue to look for an opportunity to meet in Toronto along with a small group of my Health and Wellness Team.

Thank you for providing Ms. Lalonde's timeline as requested. It was clear from the timeline that the RMCC setup and organization of the 'Draw The Line' presentation, and the unprofessional behaviour of some of the Officer Cadets lead to many of the difficulties that she experienced during her October 4, 2014 presentation. I would like to reiterate my apology for the unprofessional behaviour of select Officer Cadets, and any challenges that resulted from the setup and organization of the presentation. If not already communicated to Ms. Lalonde, I respectfully request you convey this to her at the earliest opportunity.

In reviewing the timeline, I noted several incidents that could constitute harassment under the CAF/DND Harassment Prevention and Resolution Policy. My staff is working to identify the individuals who were involved in these allegations. I would ask that you confirm with Ms. Lalonde if she can provide any identifying detail with respect to individuals who made rape jokes, cat-called or stated "I might have officer listened to you if you weren't a civilian and a woman". I appreciate that this may not be possible, but I want to ensure that we take all possible steps to address these types of behaviours. It would also be helpful if you could provide the emails that were received by the 'Draw The Line' website and the detailed email that Ms. Lalonde received. Unfortunately, if the individuals cannot be identified then it will not be possible to take administrative or disciplinary action against them. Nevertheless, as explained to you during our discussion, rest assured that corrective steps were taken against the most difficult groups.

Julie S. Lalonde: Vous etes une poubelle comme etre humain

Ce qui es vraiment triste, c'est que des femmes vous prennent comme exemple. Mais malheureusement vous n'est qu'un produit d'une société de pourri, dont vous faite partie aussi. Venir brailler devant les cameras des journalistes pour dire que vous faite des cauchemars a cause des vilains MOTS qu'on vous a dit? Mais quelle vidange de sous-humain que vous êtes.

Faible, idiote et totalement inadaptée à l'environnement. J'espère que vous rencontreriez les même victimes que je connais parce qu'elle en ont assez des opportuniste de merde comme vous. Venir dire que vous avez des séquelles... C'est dégueulasse de venir quêter de l'attention aux medias quand des dizaines de femme avec des VRAI séquelles, venant de VRAI agressions, sont sans ressources et sans support parce que des cochonneries comme vous prennent ce qui leurs reviennent. Je peux vous dire qu'elles ne vous aiment pas du tout, encore moins que les cadets...

Mais vu que votre site ressemble plus a un magasine de mode qu'un véritable engagement social.... cela veux tout dire. Heureusement votre 15 minutes de gloire est passé. Et vous retournerez à l'anonymat que vous mérité.

Je ne vous considère même pas comme une femme alors pas besoin de penser que je suis misogyne. J'ai ma copine qui est 100 fois plus forte qu'une cochonnerie comme vous. Elle je la respecte, et vous, vous pouvez aller vous pendre, triste personne sans habilités utile pour la société.

And then Xavier died.

Aftermath

IT WAS A SWELTERING LATE-SUMMER DAY. I WAS STAND-ing at a busy transit station during the evening rush hour, sweating off my TV makeup. The military had done something stupid in regard to sexual violence again, so I had spent most of the day giving my hot take in media interviews. Taylor and I had made plans to sob together at the new Amy Winehouse documentary at the hipster cinema downtown.

Bored and boiling, I aimlessly scrolled through my phone to keep myself occupied. I logged on to Facebook and saw a message from an old friend from high school. Madeleine and I had been really tight as teens and had stayed friends, albeit more casually. She had gotten married and had kids; I'd moved away. But we'd stayed friendly and I always thought fondly of her. She was one of the few people from back home who'd believed me. Everyone else bought Xavier's lie that I was a crazy ex-girlfriend who painted him as abusive for...I don't know what reason. But the lie stuck, and so I'd had to cut out most of my friends for fear they were playing both sides and telling Xavier of my whereabouts.

Madeleine had believed me when I told her why I left him, and she was one of the few people to listen to me vent about how his abuse had affected me. We didn't interact often, mostly just to comment on each other's photos, so I was surprised to see a direct message from her. I pulled into the shadow of a bus shelter so I could shield my phone from the sun and read it easier.

"Hi, Julie. I'm really sorry if this upsets you but I thought you should know. Xavier died in a car accident this morning."

I read and reread her message until my hands shook so hard, the screen was impossible to decipher.

Looking up, I saw everything in slow motion. People walking to and fro, catching a bus, hopping off one. Time stood still. It took everything I had not to grab a complete stranger's shoulder and yell, "XAVIER'S DEAD! XAVIER'S DEAD? HE'S DEAD."

I couldn't believe it.

I saw that Madeleine was still online, so I responded, "Holy fuck. Are you sure? Are you positive?"

He didn't have a common name by any means, but the news felt so unreal, I couldn't believe it.

"Yeah, it is him," she replied right away. "It's all over Facebook. All his friends and stuff. Here's a link to an OPP statement about it. I think it's in the news already, too."

I skimmed the Ontario Provincial Police article. Though it didn't have his picture, it felt like all the proof I needed that it was true.

My first instinct was to say it aloud, so I went through my phone and called everyone I knew. I tried Taylor first, since we had plans to meet up. But she must have been driving, so my call went to voicemail, where I rambled on about how I needed her to call me back right away. Only James's best friend Martin actually picked up. He had seen Xavier at peak crazy that day at the Greyhound station, and so, although he had never known him in any other light, he shared my absolute shock. A true gentleman, he asked if I needed a ride home. I told him I was going to see Taylor and that I would be fine. I tried to keep my voice down, weary of drawing attention to myself.

Taylor called me back and her sympathetic voice broke me. "Xavier's dead, Taylor. He died this morning," I repeated over and over. She offered to come get me, but my bus was arriving so it was quicker to meet her at the theatre. I boarded the bus and cried quietly the whole way there. Once I got to the theatre, I ran to Taylor, who hugged me while I wailed on her shoulder.

We agreed that watching a sad documentary about Amy Winehouse dying from bulimia and addiction was a terrible fucking idea. Instead we grabbed snacks from Whole Foods and drove back to her place. All the while, I was trying to reach James, who was driving from work to his baseball game.

Eating candy by the handful on Taylor's couch, we just kept repeating, "Xavier's dead, Xavier's dead," both of us too shocked to believe it.

The man I'd known since I was fifteen. The man I had loved for years, who broke me and kept me scared for a solid decade, had died instantly that morning in a single-vehicle crash.

The man I had tried so hard to shield from the consequences of his actions, from losing his job to getting in trouble with police, was now dead.

The man who had told me he would always love me and that I had no choice was dead.

Xavier was dead. And I couldn't believe it.

James checked his phone during the break and saw my flurry of texts and calls. I could hear the absolute shock in his voice as he repeated, "Holy fuck, holy fuck, holy fuck" into the phone.

My dad called me back too, and his shock was twofold. Xavier was young so his death was shocking. But as I yell-cried into the phone about how much the man had terrorized me,

I realized this was the first time my father was hearing the whole truth. I had shielded my parents, and most of the people in my life, from the horror show. He'd had no idea how bad things had been or that they had still been going on until his death.

James came to take me home, and I kept repeating all the way home: "Xavier's dead. Xavier's dead." I couldn't tell what I wanted more—for it to be true or a lie.

As soon as I got home, I rushed to the basement and pulled out the moss-green folder I had been carrying for the past decade. I sat on the floor and pored through every note and scrap of paper, soaking the pages with my tears. Shaking violently, I sobbed so hard, I started heaving.

To contend with my parents' separation, my mother had taken a few weeks to hike the Camino trail in Spain, and with the time difference, I knew she would be getting up soon. Worried she'd learn the news through a random Facebook post, I called her. My mother on a pilgrimage across the ocean, me on the floor of my basement. I bawled into the phone, "Ma, he's dead. Xavier died this morning." My heart was broken and I couldn't breathe.

My otherwise boisterous and energetic mom cried and spoke barely above a whisper. "It's done, Julie. You're free now."

It wasn't until this moment that I realized how much pain my loved ones had carried too. I had only given my parents tiny glimpses into the abuse Xavier put me through, but it was enough to heavily burden them. I could hear my mom buckling under the weight of the news.

I took a large dose of sleeping pills that night and lay in bed beside James, holding hands. "Do you remember what happened this morning?" he asked.

I had no idea what he was talking about.

"At like, five o'clock this morning, you sat straight up in bed and started hyperventilating. I assumed it was just a nightmare, so I pulled you back into bed and you went right back to sleep.

When you were talking to your mom, I looked up the news about Xavier. That was the exact time the accident happened."

. . .

WHEN XAVIER DIED, I WENT NUMB.

The day after, I lay on the carpeted floor of my office and wept to Nina Simone's "I Wish I Knew How It Would Feel to Be Free," a song I had long adored. It now strikes me as Peak White Lady, but at the time, every beautiful, agonizing note of that song felt like it was written for that very moment.

I was by all accounts finally free, but I couldn't feel it. I just wanted someone to tell me what freedom felt like.

Like a true millennial, I took my pain to the internet, launching into a Twitter tirade about the big, fat decade-long secret I no longer had to carry. I wanted people to understand that if this could happen to someone like me, someone with the privilege and platform to take on the Canadian Armed Forces, then you truly have no idea what people are going through unless you ask. The thread went viral and, the next day, I (stupidly) agreed to a series of radio interviews.

Sitting in Ottawa's CBC studio, I spoke live on air to a journalist I had talked to countless times before. Shell-shocked and a million miles away from my body, I went through the motions of the interview, never once believing a word that came out of my mouth. The journalist rightfully focused on the angle that I was a known advocate for victims and, meanwhile, had been a victim myself the whole time. What does that say, he wanted to know, about women isolated in their homes without a public platform to stand on?

I knew the interview was an important learning opportunity, so I put myself through the paces and said all the right things. But I could tell that he was getting frustrated. He was leading me down a path where I could conclude that Xavier's death signalled intense relief. But I wouldn't, couldn't, do it. I didn't feel relieved. I felt like a gaping wound, oozing pain all over the floor.

I left the studio to do another interview over the phone. Standing on the sidewalk outside of the CBC building, I spoke to a kind AM talk radio host about the prevalence of stalking and how isolated victims are by the very nature of the crime. Talking about stalking only makes it worse. Stalkers *want* their victims to acknowledge them. Stalkers want to know they're getting under their victims' skin, occupying their minds, being kept in their thoughts. So to stand up and talk about it is to draw more attention. This attention can be lethal.

I was in deep pain, but I pushed through the interviews, keeping my voice steady and professional. I later found out that Xavier's family called the stations to complain about my interviews, while refusing to give their names. I never named him. They don't live in my community. I have no idea how they knew I was giving those interviews.

My first therapy appointment after Xavier's death was several layers of awkward. After finally opening up about the reality that I had a stalker ex-boyfriend, we had come to the conclusion that my only way forward was to accept that it was never going to end. So imagine Dr. Lynn's surprise the following session when I roll in like, "So, funny story..." She was aghast.

The Twitter thread continued to pick up steam, and I was approached by the *Globe and Mail* to do an interview connecting my experience to the proposed new sexual health curriculum in Ontario schools. I had mentioned in my lengthy rant that the new curriculum contained content on boundaries and the importance of respecting the wishes of others, even if they break up with you.

Zosia Bielski from the *Globe* was kind and considerate, and the interview was painless. Because I was speaking as an advocate as much as from personal experience, it was easier to slip into work mode and not let my feelings rise to the surface. She mentioned that they wanted to run a photo alongside the story and set me up to meet with a photographer the next day. Since I don't let anyone know where I live, we agreed to meet at the University of Ottawa campus, where I would be in meetings that day. The photographer asked me to bring along "any artifacts" I thought would link well to the story.

For several takes, I posed on a couch outside an auditorium on the university's campus. It was a bright, sunny day, and I focused on how I should have stuck to my first choice of wearing fun heels, since the photographer ended up taking full-body photos. My last-minute decision to choose sensible espadrilles instead of leopard-print heels haunted me as I posed with a handwritten note from Xavier, promising to always love me. It was silly to care about the shoes, but obsessing over that small detail kept me from feeling the gravity of what I was doing.

That weekend, I rushed to the gas station near my house and picked up a copy. Seeing a full-page colour photo of my hands holding that note, fingers decked out in leftover yellow nail polish from the Pride parade the weekend before, made me gasp. I was still in shock, and seeing Xavier's death spelled out in one of Canada's largest newspapers, I felt like I was hearing the news for the first time again. I flipped the page and saw a half-page photo of me, side profile, trying so hard to look stoic. Putting the paper on the passenger's seat, I gripped the steering wheel with both hands and wailed. After a few minutes, I checked my makeup, blew my nose, took a deep breath, and drove to brunch with friends, never mentioning a thing.

The story continued to get traction, and I was approached by an editor at *Flare* magazine to write a lengthy piece about my experience. She gave me complete creative control, two thousand words, and a flexible deadline. The word count was three times longer than I was used to, and I dreaded the idea of writing that much. One night, I finally set my mind to it and told myself not to overthink. I have a tendency to write, delete, and rewrite the same sentence several times. (Ask me how long it took to write this fucking book!) But I told myself to go full Jack Kerouac and just stream-of-consciousness that shit. I wrote 5,500 words in one sitting.

Working with the *Flare* editorial team, I got it down to a reasonable word limit. It was for digital publication, so I got a heads-up when it was going live. The response was overwhelming and immediate. I was flooded with stories from women who'd had similar experiences. For the first time in my career, I also heard from plenty of men whose partners had "crazy ex-boyfriends just like that."

A Hollywood A-lister sent me a message on Twitter, telling me she was being stalked by an ex and was consumed with rage on the daily because it wasn't safe for her to talk about it. She thanked me for my story and told me to stay in touch. I heard from current and former members of Parliament who were being stalked by ex-husbands, ex-boyfriends, and men they had politely rejected. All of them ached that they couldn't use their platform to raise awareness about stalking and were grateful for my voice.

Denial had been my coping mechanism for a solid ten years. It was no longer possible when everyone and their neighbour was asking me about my story. As the kids would say, people were *shook* and wanted so badly to tell me what parts of my story haunted them the most. "I can't believe he moved into the apartment behind your house. That's fucking wild!" said the guy managing the radio station where I volunteered once a week. "'I will always love you, you have no choice' is some horror movie shit. Like, man. So scary!" said the former colleague I ran into at a coffee shop.

I could have told them to shut the fuck up. I could have flipped every table in sight while yelling, "You don't have to tell me! It was *my* fucking life. I'm well aware, thank you!"

But I felt responsible for upsetting people. I took on the emotional labour of caring for people who were distraught by my story. The role of supportive advocate was one I knew well. I wasn't used to getting support of my own and feared that if I sat in my feelings, I would fall apart. So I pushed them aside and wore my Julie-the-Professional hat, always the listening ear to others.

Friends did try and reach out, checking in to see how I was doing. They knew I was a frequent target for trolls, so a story like the one I'd written was sure to attract them in droves. Overall, the *Flare* article was well received, but I did get a lot of trolls who thought I had made the whole thing up for attention. ("Wasn't she just a victim at RMC? This bitch is always making herself out to be the victim.") Others went straight for the gut and told me they wished Xavier had killed me.

There was also a subset of people who didn't strike me as outright trolls but who seemed especially repulsed by the fact that I was speaking ill of the dead. Western culture doesn't contend with death very well. It's especially upsetting when you're talking about the death of a young white man. This particular crop of folks thought my story had merit, but although I never named Xavier, it was insensitive and cruel of me to speak about the situation without giving him a chance to defend himself. Apparently innocent until proven guilty applies to post-mortem discussions of an anonymous person's actions outside a court of law. Who knew.

Lots of people meant well but had such a hard time wrapping their head around what had happened to me. They saw my story and then held it up against the "successful" life I had built for myself and couldn't reconcile the two. Traumatized people don't win awards, get graduate degrees, and build a life in the public sphere. Traumatized people don't take on the Canadian Armed Forces or a university president. I didn't drink, let alone use hard drugs. I didn't self-harm, didn't develop an eating disorder, and didn't take up gambling. I didn't make reckless decisions or alienate everyone around me.

I coped by staying busy and trying to help as many women as possible. I coped by going beyond my limits and never, ever stopping. As my indigestion went to shit and my brain exploded with countless migraines, I sucked back medicine and got back out there. Occasionally my mom would check in to say, "Why are you working so hard?" and express concern about my health. But otherwise, everyone around me rewarded me for my hard work. The validation that I was doing the right thing and really, truly helping people helped me justify the unsustainable grind. "See? I can't stop. People need me."

I cared deeply about my work (and still do!) and couldn't imagine doing anything else. But I didn't do the work because I wanted to. I didn't even do it for the meagre paycheque. I did it to try and calm the raging fire in my belly that would never let me quit. I worked to end violence against women every day because I was consumed by a hunger that was never satiated.

It was the richest irony that, when I finally came out about my years of trauma, that pain was dismissed by people who refused to accept how someone who was traumatized could be in pain and *still* get shit done. My resilience was used to erase my pain.

Some friends made an effort to reach out, and although I was appreciative, I was still unable to be real. I was so used to stoicism, denial, and repression that my body was completely frozen. I spoke about Xavier in an almost zombie-like state. It was a real thing that had happened, but to a different version of me, another person, at another time.

Burying my feelings worked during the day. But every night, I came back home to face nightmares and that damn moss-green folder. I became obsessed with the idea that the folder, with all of Xavier's notes and letters inside, carried some kind of woo-woo energy that I needed to get the fuck out of my house.

Luckily, my friends and I ended every summer with one last visit to James's cottage. It dawned on me that I could burn every shred of that folder and finally rid myself of Xavier's vibes. Ever concerned about upsetting my friends, I checked in with folks first. They thought it was a brilliant idea.

Knowing full well that my story would always be met with skepticism, James and I snuck into his office afterhours and painstakingly scanned every page of the folder, keeping the results on a USB drive, lest I ever needed proof. I looked away as I scanned each page, and James blabbered at me non-stop to keep me distracted. He labelled every file "Julie is Awesome" and made me walk away as he sorted them. I came home and promptly buried the USB key in a drawer.

Standing in the driveway of James's cottage that weekend, I did a live radio interview with an infamous Toronto shock jock who had read my story and thought it was fascinating. After giving me a minute to briefly tell the story, he responded that he didn't want to seem victim-blamey, but he was curious what deficiency I had that made Xavier target me. I was ready to burn the folder, and the patriarchy, to the ground.

Later that night, as people settled in by the fire, grabbing drinks and mingling, I quietly began going through every note and burning them one by one. Slowly, my friends gathered around and quietly bore witness to what I was doing. Before I tossed it into the fire, I read out a short description or passage from each note. For one night, I was no longer concerned about how my trauma affected them. I wanted my friends to bear witness to the pain I had carried throughout my twenties. And they did. After I had gone through every document, I stood up and jubilantly tossed the folder itself into the fire. We all cheered.

I still didn't believe Xavier was truly dead and refused to dig deep into my feelings. But for one evening, I felt seen. I was surrounded by friends who had only ever known me after I broke up with Xavier, and it was incredibly validating to have them hold space for me to acknowledge what his death meant for me.

September always feels like the beginning of a new year, though I had been out of school a while by then. Old habits die hard, I guess. It had been one hell of a year. Xavier died after I'd already spent months reeling from my parent's divorce, my post-Ghomeshi workload, and the fallout from my day at RMC. I was fucking exhausted.

But I didn't have the luxury of paid vacation or sick days. I was single-handedly running a provincial campaign, and demand was through the roof. That contract had gone down to part-time, so I had also picked up a full-time contract in Renfrew County, requiring four-hour round trips to the rural area in the Ottawa Valley to interview sexual assault survivors for a needs assessment. Like every other millennial, I had never known the luxury of a permanent job. I only knew how to hustle.

So I continued to grind it out, working more and more hours and trying with all my might to keep my brain busy. Chronic, debilitating migraines would slow me down, but I would only yield, never brake. I once gave a media interview while lying on the floor of my bathroom, lights out, head by the toilet, lest another wave of migraine-induced nausea made me puke.

It was absurd, unhealthy, and unsustainable. But I knew nothing else. So I kept going.

Mid-September, I was asked to speak at a breakfast event in Ottawa to discuss workplace sexual harassment. The other panellist was Lieutenant-General Christine Whitecross, then lead on Operation HONOUR, the military's mission to address sexual violence within its ranks. Tensions were still high between me and the Canadian Armed Forces, so I knew they were none too pleased that I was added to the bill. The military demanded a pre-event phone call where I was instructed to only answer the questions put in front of me and to stick to generalizations and not personal stories or anecdotes. I laughed.

The day of this breakfast event coincided with Renfrew County's Take Back the Night March, where I had been asked to speak. Held in communities across the globe since the seventies, the events bring women and girls together to literally take back the streets as a form of protest against a culture that tells us it's unsafe to leave our houses. Since I had come out about my story just a few months prior and was known in the community, they thought mine would be the perfect survivor story to drive home the importance of the annual event. I was honoured but nervous about telling my story in front of an audience for the first time. Although radio interviews had live audiences, they weren't staring you in the face as you shouted your story from a megaphone on a street corner. But the community was always kind and supportive, so I kept telling myself I had to survive the hellish breakfast on sexual harassment and then I could decompress on my drive to Renfrew County.

I woke up painfully early, put on a fancy dress and heels, and made my way downtown to the Rideau Club. I was not sad to see that I towered over everyone who was there from the military. It's a petty power move that I love. #SorryNotSorry

The breakfast went off without a hitch. It was nice to see the Forces folks relax once they realized I wasn't interested in centring them in the conversation. With the Jian Ghomeshi story, so much had come to light about workplace sexual harassment that there was no shortage of things to talk about.

I left the event and popped into Starbucks, where I quick-changed into my activist clothes and grabbed a soy chai latte for the road. I put on my favourite EDM playlist and enjoyed the gorgeous late-September weather as I drove the two hours to Pembroke.

When I pulled into the parking lot of the Women's Sexual Assault Centre of Renfrew County, I was immediately met at my door by a colleague. "Grab your stuff and come inside," she said frantically. Confused, I gathered up my purse and megaphone and followed her inside. "Did you hear on the news?" she asked me.

I shook my head, and she proceeded to tell me that we were under lockdown. There was an active shooter on the loose, and the police had initiated a manhunt. Since this was the home of Canada's largest military base, we initially assumed it was a soldier inflicted with PTSD who had gone off.

But the small-town chatter started trickling in and we heard that it wasn't a military guy at all, but rather a civilian with a deep hatred of women. That's when we were notified that the women's centre in particular could be in danger. As one of the few explicitly feminist spaces in the county, we were a potential target.

We sat on couches, away from the windows, and chattered endlessly, trying to pass the time and ignore the reality of what was going on. Then a text message came in and we had a name. The shooter was Basil Borutski. He had killed at least two women. One of my colleagues gasped at the news and fled the room to make a frantic phone call.

We kept waiting for the news that he had killed himself, because that's the most common ending to these incidents. We sat, stewed, and pieced together what we could from texts. I had no other connections in the area besides my colleagues, so I scanned the news on my phone.

By mid-afternoon, Basil was arrested and Carol Culleton, Anastasia Kuzyk, and Nathalie Warmerdam were dead. All three women had dated Basil at one point and both Anastasia and Nathalie had reported his abuse to police.

Carol had just retired. Anastasia was a beloved real estate agent. Nathalie was a mother of two who had been working with the OPP to address police responses to violence against women. She had security cameras, a panic button, and a shotgun under her bed because she lived in fear of Basil every day.

All three women were killed in the span of two hours by a man who had once claimed to love them. I didn't know any of the women, but my colleagues did. They also knew Basil. We were shell-shocked but also had a decision to make.

Take Back the Night was scheduled for just a few short hours later. On the one hand, it was the ideal time for people to come together and condemn violence against women. But we also had no idea if Basil had acted alone, and the idea of bringing that many women out into the streets felt like putting a target on their backs. We decided to postpone for a week just to be safe. The irony was not lost on us. We were cancelling an event on violence against women because of a heinous act of violence against women.

With the event cancelled, my day was technically done. I was too shaken up to start the drive so I took to Twitter, calling on folks to pay attention to what was happening in this tiny community outside of Ottawa. Media started calling and my colleagues were grateful for something tangible to do.

I drove home in shock, and it took me hours to fall asleep. I did a media interview on CBC national television the next day. It pains me to watch the clip. Close your eyes and listen, and I'm incredibly on point. But open your eyes and I'm so visibly distraught, with frizzy hair and little makeup, trying with all my might to stay in my body and get through the interview.

I didn't know Carol, Nathalie, and Anastasia. Or even Basil. So I couldn't figure out why I was so damn upset. I mean, it's objectively terrible to be on lockdown. It's objectively terrible to hear of three women being murdered. But I felt it on a level that didn't match up with the reality of being a visitor in the community. I couldn't sleep and would spontaneously start crying, at one point even trying to fake a smile at the grocery store cashier while tears streamed down my face. The cashier was polite but horrified.

A week later, I came back to the women's centre, prepared to tell my story to a community in deep pain. One of my colleagues, Danika, was a close friend of Nathalie's. When she greeted me at the door, I was in awe of her stoicism. I arrived hours before the event to help set up and to do a check-in with everyone. As we unpacked how we were doing, I fumbled through leading the check-in, feeling guilty for being so upset when I had no personal connection to the story. Danika turned to me and said, "This is hard for you because it was your worst nightmare for ten years. What happened to them could have happened to you, and your body knows it." Later, my voice shook as I held my megaphone and projected my story into the streets of Pembroke.

The county held a number of vigils in different communities. I attended as many as I could, breaking down each time. The sight of elderly women, children, young moms, and rural men with trucker hats openly sobbing broke my heart in a way I had never thought possible.

The community of Petawawa has a memorial for women who have been victims of male violence. The monument went up years before the triple femicide, but eerily, it consists of three women carved out of wrought iron. At the Petawawa vigil, I was asked to read a short poem but had to stop several times to catch my breath. The whole thing felt so foretold. It destroyed me.

Everyone who heard my story wanted me to punctuate it with "but he's dead so I'm totes cool now, folks!" I was so sad that I couldn't. Everyone saw freedom and peace, but I was stuck in confusion. Why was I spared and Nathalie, Carol, Anastasia—and countless other women—weren't?

Although Dr. Lynn was doing her best to get me to thaw from my years of repression and denial, I felt like the paltry amount of progress I had made went out the window. The triple femicides of September 22, 2015, sent me further into overwork and running myself thin. I had been so confused in my own feelings about Xavier's death. Hearing from the friends and family of three incredible women who had not survived,

I felt immense pressure to make something of myself.

I had survived something that was statistically impossible. Stalking kills. Domestic violence kills. Ontario's Domestic Violence Death Review Committee has a list of red flags for a woman experiencing domestic violence who is at risk of homicide. I met nearly all the criteria. I should not have survived. Yet, I was here. Countless women weren't. The burden felt unbearable.

So I threw myself into work and tried to keep my head up. But despite my best efforts, I was slowly overcome with crippling depression. I missed countless deadlines because I slept for hours every night and needed a nap every afternoon. I lost my appetite. I cried at random intervals or was unbelievably irritable. I had no patience, no energy, and no desire to do anything.

I kept up a facade and made up excuses for my late work, and few people seemed to catch on. I did interviews in bed, in a towel on the floor of the bathroom, or lying on the couch. My showers would last almost an hour, as I'd sit in the tub and let the water hit me in the face, hoping it would help me feel anything. I got a tattoo across my ribs, a notoriously painful spot, and to the awe of the artist, literally fell asleep.

I was plagued with nightmares that Xavier had faked his death just to fuck with me. In the dreams, I would notice that he was watching me and when I would confront him, he'd laugh in my face. "Who's going to believe you? You sound crazy," he would sneer. I would wake up in a cold sweat and struggle to fall back asleep.

I developed what I affectionately called "zombie arms." Waking up one night, I discovered that I was lying flat on my back with my arms straight up in the air, like a zombie in some corny horror movie. Confused, I put my arms down and fell back asleep. Far from a one-off, I started rocking zombie arms almost every night. But rather than just holding my arms up, I started running my fingernails down my forearms in a soft, sweeping motion. James would periodically wake up to the sound of my long acrylic nails scratching against my skin and would gently pull my arms down, all while I remained completely asleep.

Mortified at my bizarre nightly ritual, I brought it up to my therapist. Like a true professional, she didn't judge. She approached it with curiosity. "Do you wake up panicked or anxious on those nights, like you do usually?" she asked.

I realized for the first time that it was my body's subconscious attempt to soothe me. Like part of my brain activated my nightmare and the other part would jump in and say, "There, there" and try to calm my body down.

"Every part of you wants to heal, Julie," Dr. Lynn insisted. "Even when you're dead asleep, your body is fighting to keep you safe." Maybe I was making some progress after all.

But in my waking hours, I didn't feel better. As the days, weeks, and months passed after Xavier's death, I hated myself more and more for not being well. I was supposed to be free. I was supposed to be happy. Why couldn't I just snap out of it? I diligently made all my therapy appointments, worked out regularly, ate healthy, took my vitamins, and wanted so badly to be better. But I was feeling discouraged. "Xavier is dead. Why doesn't it feel over?" I pleaded to Dr. Lynn, hoping for some magical advice that would solve all my problems.

She calmly leaned over, looked me in the eye, and said, "Xavier's dead, but he's not dead *to you.*"

The truth hit me square in the face. As my friend Taylor pointed out to me one night as I cried on her couch, I had been in a relationship with Xavier since I was fifteen. We had been friends for three years and dated for two years, and then he stalked me for ten. I didn't consent to most of that relationship, but it was nonetheless a relationship. And just like a regular breakup after that many years, this would also take time to heal.

To release Xavier, I had to release the younger version of

myself that I would no longer get to be. I left Xavier when I was twenty. He died when I was thirty. He robbed me of some of the best years of my life. A solid decade where I watched others backpack through Europe, hook up with babes they met at bars, and take risk after risk. I did none of those things. I spent those years on borrowed time, trying to accomplish as much as I could, feeling like the clock was ticking. Ten years of my life that I will never get back.

I realized that so much of the pain I carried was for my younger self. I didn't miss Xavier, but I missed who we were when we were young. I missed that wild summer when we had the whole world ahead of us and saw only potential. I missed being young, beautiful, vibrant, and full of energy. I had big dreams and felt invincible. That innocent, carefree young woman I was is dead. She's never coming back.

To let go of Xavier, I had to let her go too.

Julie S. Lalonde, summer 1985–summer 2015

It is with a mixture of grief and relief that we announce the death of Julie S. Lalonde. A daughter, sister, auntie, partner, and friend, she will be remembered for her potty mouth, debilitating night terrors, and commitment to women's rights. Julie dreamed of becoming a writer and, as a middle-schooler, wrote an essay about her ideal adulthood as a famous author who lived alone with several cats. She wanted to travel the world and write the stories of every interesting person she met. Instead, she suffered from crippling anxiety and depression and coped by spending every waking hour trying to end violence against women. Internet trolls would be surprised to know that she was voted funniest person of her graduating class. Although her dreams of adventure and shenanigans were never realized, her friends and family would like you to know that she never lost her sense of humour. She was a woman of contradictions who didn't believe in God or "any of that hippie-dippy shit," but she did believe in karma and reincarnation. Those of us who knew her best are hopeful that in her next life, she is given the freedom to fulfill her dreams.

In keeping with Julie's wishes, we ask that you make a donation to your local women's shelter and commit to punching every rapist in the dick.

8
Carte Blanche

WHEN YOUR DEPRESSION IS UNBEARABLE AND YOU'RE
mourning the younger part of yourself whose potential will
never be realized, may I suggest throwing a party? If it doesn't
work, at least you still get to dance around and eat some
snacks.

The act of my friends holding space by a campfire was one
of the few things that had broken my feelings of isolation.
I didn't know anyone else who had been stalked like I had.
I didn't know anyone whose abuser had died. I had no community. But that night by the fire, I felt connected. I felt seen. I felt
loved for the person I *was*, not the person I could have been.
My friends didn't see me as broken, nor did they see me as the
stoic warrior who could handle anything. I wasn't an advocate
or a Twitter profile. I was a human being who had survived
something heinous. And that was okay.

In a last-ditch effort to make my newfound freedom feel
real, I decided to throw a party. I love a good dance party, and it
felt ideal to be surrounded by supportive friends with no obli-

gation to tell my whole story while sobbing. Julie's Freedom Party was to be a night replete with dancing, candy, and celebration. I wasn't happy Xavier was dead, but I longed to be happy to be alive. And that was worth celebrating.

My closest friends jumped at the idea. I pulled together freedom-based snacks like Give Peas a Chance and Freedom Fries. I curated a playlist with the most on-point bangers, namely most of the Destiny's Child discography and George Michael's "Freedom! '90." I bought a fat Cuban cigar and got my favourite party dress dry-cleaned.

As the date approached, I checked in with people who had yet to RSVP. Frankly, in the grand scheme of what I was entitled to ask for, "Come to my house and party with me" felt like an easy ask. By everyone's account, I was having a rough go, and so I didn't think it was too much to ask to swing by my house party.

But more than one friend was repulsed by the idea. "It's in bad taste," one friend told me over text. Another ignored my messages and told me a few weeks later that they bailed because they thought the whole idea was morbid and made them uncomfortable.

I was hurt and embarrassed. Was I being morbid? Was it cruel? Was I asking too much?

I mean, I recognized it was a fucked-up situation. "Hey, my ex-boyfriend/stalker just died in an accident, and as a result, I feel like I died too, so wondering if you're free on Saturday to get drunk and dance around my house to early 2000s hip-hop?" Not a huge ask in practical terms, but it did require people be *very* chill about death and grief.

My embarrassment turned to anger. I was tired of carrying everyone else's feelings about *my* pain. I never want to force someone to be uncomfortable, but to deny the importance of the party was to deny what Xavier had done to me. It was a denial of my pain and trauma.

I wanted so badly to perform my healing in a way that made sense to other people. But Xavier never apologized to me. He'll never be held accountable. I couldn't attend Xavier's funeral. I have no grave to visit. I had to make my own ritual and find my own way to grieve. Having lived with a secret for so long, I desperately needed people to bear witness. To deny me that felt like betrayal.

So I threw a party. As I danced the night away with my friends and ate candy until my mouth felt raw, I would stop momentarily and approach the closest person to me with the same question. "Xavier's dead, right? He's really dead?" And they would kindly, patiently respond, "Yeah, girl. He's dead."

Outside, smoking my celebratory cigar, I turned to one friend and said, "Hey! Did you know Xavier's dead?" and he nodded and then poured a shot onto the sidewalk. "Yup. Let's pour one out for that homie."

Midway through the party, my friends pulled out a piñata. James gingerly held it as I whacked and whacked at a giant Darth Vader head while my friends cheered me on.

I wanted to end the night with a short speech, expressing my deep gratitude for everyone who had come out to participate in my unorthodox grieving ritual. But I found myself truly emotional for the first time all night, so I ended with a quick "Thank you so much. This means so much to me. And I know it's a weird ask, and I know a lot of people aren't here because it's sort of a fucked-up request, so please know I appreciate you." And before I could start sobbing, James lit up a bunch of sparklers. We danced around my living room, choking on the smoke of too many sparklers in a tight space (oops!) while Ice Cube's "You Can Do It" blared.

That night, I slept soundly for the first time in years.

Ellipsis

I TRAVEL THE COUNTRY NOW, TALKING TO PEOPLE ABOUT what I've lived through.

I still deny audiences a clean ending to my story.

I still get death threats. My mom still wants me to find another job.

I'm still jumpy. I still hate crowds. I sleep with the curtains drawn and don't advertise where I live.

I no longer deny how much it affects me. I'm no longer interested in looking tough, stoic, or resilient. I'm not interested in feeding the narrative that I'm a superwoman who can handle anything.

I am not more resilient than Rehtaeh Parsons or Nathalie Warmerdam or Carol Culleton or Anastasia Kuzyk or any of the other women and girls whose lives were stolen by misogynists. I just got lucky.

I'm not interested in individual stories of survival.

I want to see us kick down the systems that force us to fight so hard in the first place.

I want us all to make it.

I want to make it.

Acknowledgements

WRITING A BOOK IS REALLY FUCKING HARD AND IF ANY-one tells you otherwise, cut them out of your life because you don't need that kind of bullshit.

Thank you to the Ontario Arts Council for providing me with funding that allowed me to retreat to the Banff Centre on two separate occasions so I could excavate my bones and extract all the stories necessary for this book to be written.

Thank you to Amanda Crocker for listening to me give a talk about workplace sexual harassment and thinking, *This woman has a story to tell.* I am incredibly grateful for your trust and patience.

Thank you to Michael Orsini for thinking it was perfectly rational that I got asked to write a book. Thanks for the vegan BLT dates and for appreciating what a nice pair of shoes can do to one's mood.

Thank you to Tilman Lewis for your detailed edits. (You're literally editing the grammar of my acknowledgement of your greatness!) Writing from a place of a trauma, in my second language, means you were given a bit of a mess. Thanks for your help.

Thank you to Ingrid Paulson for the stunning cover and layout. You took a disturbing stack of documents and were able to show the readers what it feels like to constantly be interrupted and derailed. I'm in awe of your brilliance.

Thank you to Tracey Lindeman for being an early reader who gave me the best real-talk feedback and detailed edits. Thanks for letting me cry on your couch with Piet when everything felt like too much.

Thank you to Maureen Halushak, who was the first to believe in my writing and allowed me to "come out" in a fashion magazine, which is truly all this femme ever wanted.

Thank you to all the amazing writers I had the honour of hanging with at the Banff Centre. Special thanks to Alex Leslie, who was my mentor and the first person to ever read a single page of this book. You made me feel like I just might be able to do this. Thank you to Cherie Dimaline, who not only wrote one of my favourite books of all time, but whose mentorship at the Banff Centre also helped me stand in my power. Un gros merci to David Bradford for letting me pick your brilliant mind on what to do with all the archival material I had. Thank you to Ali Pinkney for holding space for me when I was *very* in my feelings. Thank you to Shawk Alani for letting me be vulnerable and for laughing at all my jokes. Thank you to Elizabeth Aiossa for nurturing all the dark parts of my psyche. I love you.

Milles mercis to the real Dr. Lynn, James, Taylor, Martin, Madeleine, and all the amazing friends I've made in the years since the old me died. Please don't read this book.

Finally, I want to thank Rihanna. Just because.

JULIE S. LALONDE is an internationally recognized women's rights advocate and public educator. Julie works with various feminist organizations dedicated to ending sexual violence, engaging bystanders and building communities of support. She is a frequent media source on issues of violence against women and her work has appeared on *Al Jazeera*, CBC's The National, TVO's The Agenda, Vice, *WIRED* magazine and *FLARE*, among others. She is a recipient of the Governor General's Award in Commemoration of the Persons Case.